Love's Touch

EUNICE PORTER

Table of Contents

PREFACE

During the Apostle Paul's second missionary journey, he was led by the Holy Spirit to Corinth, which was a port city on a narrow bridge of land connecting mainland Greece with the Peloponnesian peninsula. Corinth was a city notorious for its licentious lifestyle, no doubt encouraged by the worship of Venus, goddess of sensual lust. Her temple housed a thousand professional prostitutes!

Paul spent eighteen months in Corinth (Acts 18:1-7), and a large Church was born, as people turned to Christ in response to his Gospel message of the cross of Christ (50 – 51 A.D.) But after Paul moved on, the news of some disturbing problems in the Church reached him in Ephesus. The book we know as 1st. Corinthians is one of the letters he wrote to them, to deal with the issues. Some of the things he addressed were difficult and controversial, even to this day.

So a couple of years ago, when God laid it on my heart to write a book as a study of this letter, I balked at the idea. I felt totally inadequate to make sense of either the issues themselves, or of Paul's reaction and response. And how was it relevant to the Church culture today? Reluctantly, I started going through the first few chapters, trying to sort out the topics and organize them as I took notes. However, my heart was really not in it! Eventually I put it on the back burner, and focused on another book: "Kingdom Lessons from the Fabric of Life" (pub. 2014).

Several months ago, with the other book published, printed and ready to go, I was awakened one morning at 4:00 a.m. with what turned out to be a nudging nod from God. My head was full of words, pictures and ideas; and more kept coming! Grabbing a notepad and pen, I began writing down what I was hearing, not grasping immediately what was happening. Then the flow stopped, and suddenly I knew! This was the key to my dilemma, the catalyst to begin writing, and the confidence I needed to tackle a difficult task, with the leading of the Holy Spirit. God had so gently confirmed His plan for me, and I knew I could trust Him to guide me along the way, since He entrusted me to do it.

And so the book grew and took form inside me, with those seeds planted in my mind and spirit becoming the springboard for action, the theme of the first chapter, and the focus of the book you now read. Interestingly, as I worked through the issues that Paul faced, I felt that I shared some of his feelings of frustration, disappointment and displeasure, tempered with a deep love for God's people and a desire to see them walking in the Truth, and filled with the fullness of His grace and blessing. As you read, I trust that God's love will shine through Paul's words as well as mine, as we share His heart for His people – YOU!

DEDICATION

I have spent much time over the past several months commiserating with the Apostle Paul in his vexation, exasperation and sorrow as he encountered some un-Christ-like attitudes and behavior in a Church he had 'planted', prayed for and parented as a loving father. In the process, I have found myself becoming much more sympathetic towards the 'shepherds of the flock' who face similar issues in these days. Even though I could not completely identify with Paul as a pastor, as a writer I felt some of his frustration, just trying to interpret how it all relates to us in today's Church.

I have depended on the Holy Spirit to guide me through the 'building' of this book, and know how important it is for all pastors to be filled with the Holy Spirit as they implant the Truth of God's Word into the lives under their care, and are faithful stewards of this Truth. Thus, **I dedicate this book to you who are Church pastors,** with the hope that you will be encouraged to walk humbly and lovingly in your calling, not daunted by the problems among the sheep, but fully equipped to meet them with the wisdom and counsel of the Holy Spirit. In this you will be blessed and a blessing, for God's glory!

STUDY ONE

A study on Paul's letter to the Church at
Corinth, known today as First Corinthians

By this we know love,
because He laid down His life for us.
1 John 3:16

Behold what manner of love the Father
has bestowed on us, that we should
be called children of God!
1 John 3:1

1 THE SECRET TREASURE

(And the hidden key)

Imagine with me that we have found a very old box, affixed with the broken seal of the Apostle Paul, and labeled "Corinth". In the manner of writing in the first century A.D., we find a number of scrolls, tied together in bundles, with twine. There's quite a large group marked "Issues to Address". Hmmm! We blow off the dust and remove the spider webs, to find articles on "Nasty Behavior", "Clashing Cultures", "Division", "Dissension", and "Controversial Doctrines". Obviously these files haven't been looked at in a long while. They are probably too hot to handle! You can almost feel the heat of Paul's passion burning through his words.

But wait! Not all the scrolls are dust-laden. Another group is labeled "Foundational Teaching". Here Paul writes about "Our Calling in Christ", "Apostleship", "Gifting by the Holy Spirit" and "The Resurrection". It seems that these are 'safe' subjects for a lot of people, some more so than others.

Tucked in the midst of these two piles of 'files', we find a treasure wrapped in a tiny, shiny box – 13 by 13. As we open it, we see a silver plaque engraved with words of gold. Aha! This is the jewel that has been paraded at many a wedding – and no wonder. Its words portray the beautiful qualities of marital love. (*Sigh!* If every couple who hears these words at the altar would heed them and live by them, divorce would disappear!)

Hold on a minute! This isn't talking only about marital love. It's about family love, friend love (and enemy love). It includes neighborly love, love for the unlovely, the lost and the helpless (the kind of love that Jesus often talked about). It shows how we are to love one another in the Church, world-wide. But best of all, it is an amazing description of the nature of God, who epitomizes the kind of love expressed here, because that's who He is. "God is Love" (1 John 4:16). This *"love of God has been poured out in our hearts by the Holy Spirit who was given to us"* (Rom.5:5). *"The fruit of the Spirit is love"*, in all its radiating facets of *"joy, peace, longsuffering, kindness, goodness, faithfulness, gentleness, and self-control"* (Gal.5:22-23). Please read 1 Corinthians 13!

So why is this literary gem in the middle of the confusing and weighty matters of Paul's first letter to the Christian believers in Corinth? I think we find the answer in the seven words just outside the top of the "box", and two words at the bottom. Paul introduces us to the treasure with the words, "*I show you a more excellent way*" (1 Cor.12:31), and closes with "*Pursue love*" (14:1).

Up to the end of chapter 12, Paul has been dealing with some serious problems that had arisen in the Church at Corinth. He's probably wondering, "Will they <u>ever</u> learn? What more can I write, that will change their selfish and worldly ways? I poured myself into their lives, and I love them like a father. But now that I've been gone for a while, they are acting like spoiled children. They're quarreling and misbehaving so badly. What's going on?"

I like to think that Paul is crying out to God, and the answer comes to Him in a gentle whisper: "<u>Remind them how much I love them</u>. When they fully receive My love, everything they do will be from a heart of love. My perfect <u>love</u> in them <u>is the answer to every relational issue</u>. It is <u>a moral compass</u> and <u>spiritual benchmark</u> for every part of their entire life."

Most of us know John 3:16, which succinctly sums up the depth of God's love for us - giving His Son to die in our place, in order to give us eternal life. But, did you know what 1 John 3:16 says about love? *"By this we know love, because He laid down His life for us. And we also ought to lay down our lives for the brethren."* This is not a selfish love that has no regard for others. It is a love that puts others before ourselves. According to 1 John and 1 Cor.13, love is often the missing ingredient in what we think, say and do. The result - we hurt people when we should be helping and healing them.

All this to advise, as we study the book of 1 Corinthians, that we approach every nasty situation from God's perspective, and through His eyes of love and forgiveness. It is not our place to judge the actions of others, but to examine our own hearts and motives (Matt.7:1-5; Rom.14:12-13; Gal.6:1-5). Judgment must be mitigated with love, and justice tempered by mercy. I realize the believers at Corinth lived long ago and far away, in a different culture; but in many ways we today face the same problems they did. Paul's letter to them is still relevant for us, so let us examine it with eyes open to see what God is saying to us through His Word.

To get our mind prepared for this bumpy journey, I ask that you do the following (after having thoughtfully read the 'Love' chapter, 1 Cor.13):

With pen and paper in hand, go through the chapter slowly, phrase by phrase, concept by concept, asking the Holy Spirit, "What are You saying to me?" As He brings understanding of the message to you, rewrite each idea/verse in your own words, receiving it and owning it. Continue this personal paraphrase through the chapter. While it is still fresh in your mind, read your paraphrased version back to yourself, asking God to impress it indelibly on your heart, as a daily reminder to walk in His love.

(Note: If you are unsure of the meaning of a word or concept, look it up in a concordance, Google it or check other versions of the text.)

(Note: If you are studying this book in a group, bring your paraphrase to the group to share. It may reveal how words of Scripture can speak to people in different ways. Although the text is different, the message is the same; but certain truths will grab each heart in an individual manner.

2 WHO CALLS?

1 Corinthians 1:1-9

Qu'Appelle, derivative of 'qui appelle', French for "Who calls?" is the name of a valley and a small town in southern Saskatchewan, taken from the legend of a young Aboriginal man, penned by E. Pauline Johnson:

"I am the one who loved her as my life,
Had watched her grow to sweet young womanhood;
Won the dear privilege to call her wife
And found the world, because of her, was good.
I am the one who heard the spirit voice,
Of which the paleface settlers love to tell;
From whose strange story they have made their choice
Of naming this fair valley the Qu'Appelle."

The word 'call' in its various forms and connotations, is used repeatedly throughout the Bible, notably so in the book of 1 Corinthians (three times in the first two verses). In the best usage of the word, a 'call' is very affirming and comforting. Think of a young child who, attracted by some new sight, wanders away from his parents in a store, or on a camping trip. It is not long before they realize he has strayed, and they begin scanning their surroundings. Fear and concern, birthed out of love for him, fill the heart and voice of the mother/father as they call out his name over and over again, frantically hoping for a glimpse of their precious one, or to hear the sound of his voice calling them!

Meanwhile, the child, oblivious of the disturbance he has caused, continues to chase the momentary pleasure until he suddenly looks up to share it with his parent . . . Now <u>he</u> panics, and he runs wildly, looking for that familiar form and face. Fear mounts in him, and he begins to call out "Mommy!" or "Daddy!" What pathos and helplessness is in that plaintive cry!

Like that child, perhaps you have wandered away from your heavenly Father; or maybe you cannot yet call Him 'Father'. In either case, God's Spirit is calling you: "*Come now, and let us reason together. Though your sins are as scarlet, they shall be as white as snow*" (Isa.1:18). "*Come to me, all you who labor and are heavy laden, and I will give you rest*" (Matt.11:28). He calls you by name, over and over, long before you ever realize you are lost! This is the call to salvation from sin. He wants to forgive you and give you new life, joy and hope in His love. He waits for you to call His name. "*Whoever calls on the name of the LORD shall be saved*" (Rom.10:12-13; 1 Cor.1:2b).

Who calls? Our Creator, God, calls us to be in His family and to be called His child! (John 1:12). 1 Cor.1:2a tells us that the Church of God is made up of people who are sanctified ("*called to be saints*"). 'Sanctified' simply means 'to be set apart for God', and separated from sin. You and I are called by God to be saints! Because of forgiveness of sin we receive a new standing before God (2 Cor.5:17) - a state/lifestyle/purpose in which we are to be pure in thought, morally blameless, devoted to worshipping God and bringing glory to Him!

If we look at other Scriptures, we get a glimpse into the broad spectrum of the call of God on us:

- 1 Cor.1:9 - we are *invited/summoned/"called into the fellowship of Jesus Christ our Lord".* This is the fellowship experienced in the Church (1:2), which is the "ecclesia", or assembly of called-out ones. (See Acts 2:42 and 1 John 1:3).
- 1 Cor.7:15b – "*God has called us to peace*": peace with God, and the peace of God (Rom.5:1; Phil.4:7).

- Eph.1:18 – *We are called <u>to hope and to the riches of His inheritance</u>.* (See 1 Pet.1:4, 3:9b; Rom.8:30).
- 1 Pet.2:9 – *God has called us <u>out of darkness into His marvelous light</u>.* (See Col.1:13).

What an amazing calling! But the calling Paul refers to in the first words of greeting in this letter is <u>a choosing by God to a particular vocation</u>, in his case that of Apostle. The word 'apostle' suggests an appointed delegate, or a chosen ambassador of the Gospel. Paul makes it clear that this wasn't <u>his</u> choice. It was the will of God – and the farthest thing from Paul's mind (Acts 9). <u>We</u> may not all be called to be Apostles, but we <u>are called to be lights and witnesses in the world</u>, of God's grace and Gospel (Matt.5:16; Acts 1:8).

<u>Grace (charis)</u> - (1 Cor. 1:3-4) Strong, in his concordance (#5485), defines the Greek word 'charis' as "the divine influence upon the heart, and its reflection in the life". It is gifts and unearned favor, lavished upon us by God, because He loves us so much! Note that <u>this grace of God to us is made possible through Christ</u> (Rom.6:23).

<u>Gifts of Grace to the Corinthian Church (vs.5-9)</u>:

- Speaking in tongues – evidence of the baptism in the Holy Spirit, promised by Christ (vs.5-6)
- All knowledge (v.5) i.e. the wisdom of God (2:6-7)
- Hope of Christ's return (v.7) – Phil.3:20
- Sustaining grace (v.8) – Jude 24
- God's faithfulness (v.9) – 1 Thes.5:24

Paul goes to great lengths here to affirm the Corinthian believers in <u>their calling to be saints, as well as their gifting by God's grace</u>. No doubt this softens the blow of his remonstrations that follow. Paul had received so much grace in his own life, and was readily willing to acknowledge the grace that had been given to these immature believers, though obviously their current behavior did not play out in grace towards others.

What can we learn from this passage as it applies to showing grace to other believers who may not measure up to our standards of commitment and conduct?

List some grace gifts that you have received since you believed. Are you working these out in daily interaction with others? If not, what do you think is the hindrance?

3 FAMILY SQUABBLES

1 Corinthians 1:10-17; 3:1-6, 21-23

No sooner did Paul affirm that the believers in Corinth had been <u>called into the fellowship of Christ</u> (1:9), than he began to show them where they were falling short of this calling. 'Fellowship' is translated from the Greek word 'koinonia', and the meaning includes agreement, communion, communication, oneness, partnership, and participation. From our text we can learn what fellowship <u>is</u> by examining what it is <u>not</u>!

- A uniform testimony = No mixed messages
- A unity of mind and purpose = No divisions
- A oneness of discernment = No contention
- Obedience to Christ only = No man-pleasers
- Maturity in Christ = No childish envy/strife

Although Paul is pointing out negative and un-Christ-like behavior among the Corinth believers, he speaks out of love, and a desire that they mature in their faith, with the understanding that because they are Christ's, they have all that they need (1:10; 3:21-23). Later on, Paul teaches on the work of the Holy Spirit to bring us into holiness and maturity. When he penned a letter to the fellowship of believers at Ephesus, his words in chapter four echo and expand on this truth. (Notice similar language to our text, in this quote): "*I. . .beseech you to <u>walk worthy of the calling with which you are called,</u> with all lowliness and gentleness, with longsuffering, <u>bearing with one another in love,</u> endeavoring to keep <u>the unity of the Spirit in the bond of peace</u> . . . till we all come to the unity of the faith, and of the knowledge of the Son of God, to a perfect man, to the measure of the stature of the fullness of Christ; that <u>we</u>*

should no longer be children" (Eph.4:1-3, 13-14). It's the same message, expressed in different words!

As we have seen in our text, one of the main sources of division in the Church body was that some people were touting Paul as their leader, while others claimed to be followers of Peter, Apollos, and even of Christ! Paul's answer to this, briefly stated in ch.3:5-6, 21, is that he and his fellow pastors were simply ministers that God used to bring the Gospel to them. They were not to be lauded and applauded for what they had been called of God to do. It was God, by His Word and Spirit, who had brought them to salvation through the message these ministers brought, and all the glory was His!

Fast forward to the twenty-first century. Are people in the Church today really completely following Christ, or are we lining up behind leaders whose teaching we prefer, almost making them our idols? We must be careful not to glorify men; and as ministers, not to take the glory which belongs to God! FOOD FOR THOUGHT

 4 FOOLISHNESS OR WISDOM?

1 Corinthians 1:18-25; 3:18-20

The debate has been ongoing for about two thousand years, and Paul's letter might well contain the first record of it! The premise for any argument is that there are at least two opposing points of view. In the case of "The Message of the Cross" in our text, the wisdom of man is pitted against the wisdom of God; and the final conclusion of the argument is that the wisdom of the world is foolishness to God. Conversely, the wisdom of God is foolishness to a man of the world. Let's listen in on Paul's debate from these two perspectives:

The message of the cross (Christ crucified) is:

- Foolishness to the perishing - 1:18
- **The power of God to believers** – 1:18; 2:5
- An offence to the Jews – 1:23, 24
- Absurdity to the Greeks – 1:23
- **The wisdom of God to the called ones** – 1:24

What is the message of the cross? Let's first examine some background information. During the reign of the Roman Empire, crucifixion, or death by hanging on a cross, was the chosen method of punishment for certain crimes. If you have ever seen movies about the passion of Christ, you know this was a most shameful, horrific, excruciatingly slow and torturous way to die!

Criminals were hung on a cross, naked, in a public place, in full view of multitudes of curious onlookers, so as to be examples/warnings to any would-be murderers, etc. The cross was the greatest demonstration of shame and suffering in the worst sense of those words. This, this, my friend, was what Jesus endured, in order to bring us life, to bring us to glory as His Bride, and to make us fellow-heirs with Him as children of the Father!

Jesus, the pure, sinless Son of God, our Creator God in human form, hung there with criminals. Nails fastened His hands and feet to a rough-hewn tree, which tore at His bruised and bloodied body with every gasp of breath He labored for. Blood covered His face as the cruel crown of thorns pierced his brow. Passersby taunted Him, to which He answered not a complaining word.

As unbelievably cruel as the physical and mental anguish of the cross was, the bruising of spirit He experienced when all the sins of all mankind were pressed upon Him, was inconceivably horrendous, and it literally broke the pure heart of this Holy One! Those who placed Him there had no idea what they had done, and were amazed to hear His tender words of forgiveness. The cross of Jesus became the greatest demonstration ever of love and redemption in the most beautiful sense of those words! It became the theme of countless hymns of praise and worship, because it was the means of bringing us out of darkness into light. At the cross, our sins were atoned for, to give us forgiveness and peace with God. It is the crux of our full and free salvation.

The apostle Paul was so convinced of the power of the cross, and its centrality to the Gospel message, that he reminded the Corinthians: "*I determined not to know anything among you except Jesus Christ and Him crucified.*" (2:2) I wonder if Paul (Saul) was in Jerusalem during the trial and crucifixion of Jesus. As a devout Jew, it is safe to say he would not miss the Passover feast. Did he witness the event that so incensed him to anger, that he became a zealous persecutor of all who believed this

Man and His *'foolish'* message? (Acts 8:1-3) Saul did not know what would soon follow (Acts 9).

Think about this: *"It pleased God by the foolishness of the message preached to save those who believe"* (1 Cor.1:21); and *"the foolishness of God is wiser than men"* (v.25). Can you attest to the fact that at one time the message of the cross was foolishness to you? Why? 2 Cor.4:4 tells us that Satan has blinded the minds of people so they cannot see the glory of Christ. But v.6 tells us: *"God . . .has shone in our hearts to give the light of the knowledge of the glory of God in the face of Jesus Christ"*. From start to finish, Salvation is God's work, not ours.

In a few verses, Paul examines the wisdom of the world, which rejects the message of the cross. He contrasts it with the power of God and sums it all up in ch.1, v.21 – *"For since, in the wisdom of God, the world through wisdom did not know God, it pleased God through the foolishness of the message preached to save those who believe."* Paul speaks from experience!

Let us look at the how the wisdom of the world stacks up in the light of God's wisdom, given to His people by the Holy Spirit (2 Tim.1:7).

The weakness of the wisdom of the world:

- Rejects the message of the cross – 1:18
- Will be destroyed by God – 1:19
- Is deemed foolish by God – 1:20; 3:19
- Does not know God – 1:21
- Is never satisfied; always seeking – 1:22
- Is deceptive and not dependable – 3:18
- Is known to God and is futile – 3:20

The Power of God's Wisdom:

- Brings salvation to all who believe – Rom.1:16
- Raised Jesus from the grave – Eph.1:19-20
- Enables us to witness for Him – Acts 1:8
- Gives us joy, peace and hope – Rom.15:13
- Works in us, giving us strength and grace – Eph.3:20, 6:10; Col.1:11; Gal.5:22-23

Do you see that the Power is the Holy Spirit?

Can you list some ways in which you have experienced the power of God in your life?

What are some things God has changed in you? (In what ways are you different than before you received Christ as your Savior?)

5   CHOSEN BY GOD

1 Corinthians 1:26-31

"*He* (the Father) *chose us* in Him (the Son) *before the foundation of the world, that we should be holy and without blame before Him in love, having predestined us to adoption as sons to Himself, according to the good pleasure of His will.*" These verses (Eph.1:4-5) open up a floodgate of glorious, amazing truth, wisdom and counsel which gush forth from the page like a cleansing, refreshing river, to uplift, purify and change us. I hope that this letter was sent to the struggling believers at Corinth! How blessed we are to have it as a part of the Word of God to us today!! It is priceless!

Was it ever your experience as a child to stand on the fringe, while others stronger and more skilled hear their names called to be on the team? How you want to be 'chosen', but you just don't measure up. Your unspoken cry "Pick me! Pick me!" dies in your throat, as you wistfully watch your friends enjoy the game. If this was you, keep reading!

In our text from the Corinthian letter, Paul switches from 'called' to 'chosen' to describe the process by which we became children of God. It is similar to the word 'predestined', which precedes the word 'called' in Romans 8:29-30. It infers a deliberate decision to send the call out to certain people. His choices might surprise us. Have you ever thought, "Why did God choose <u>me</u>?"

It seems that God had a different set of criteria for His choices than most humans would use (v.26). <u>He chose</u>:

- *Not many wise,*   BUT   <u>the foolish</u>
- *Not many mighty,* BUT   <u>the weak</u>
- *Not many noble,* BUT   <u>the insignificant</u>

It doesn't look like the makings of a great team, does it?

If I were to hazard a guess as to why God did not choose many from among 'the elite', I would say He knew that not many of the wise, mighty or noble on earth would respond to His invitation. This is not because of their achievements per se, but because these achievements blind them to the realization that they need God, or that the life He gives is so much better than what they have. The truth of the old rhyme: "Life is short; Death is sure; Sin the cause; Christ the cure" is much too simplistic and inane for them to consider.

Look at the opening words of v.26. It's almost as if Paul is teasing them with a touch of sarcasm. To paraphrase,

"My dear brothers, look around you, at all your fellow believers. You can see that not many of you have much to be proud of as far as accomplishments go. Not many are famous scholars, powerful leaders or the upper-crust sort. And yet <u>you are the ones God chose</u>!" In reality they were much like the disciples Jesus chose to follow Him and to learn His ways. <u>They</u> were a pretty motley crew, who didn't show much promise for quite some time. Like them, the Corinthian believers needed a jump start to get them ignited. More on that later!

All speculation and sarcasm aside, Paul lists some very <u>valid reasons for God's choices</u>:

1. To demonstrate to everyone, that God's wisdom, power and endowment in us is far greater than what the world has or can offer - vs.27-28

2. So that none of us can boast in our own wisdom, strength or status - v.29
3. So we will glory in God alone (that He will get the glory for everything we are, have or do) – v.31

Vs.30 – <u>Jesus became for us, and is our</u>:

- <u>Wisdom from God</u> (by the Holy Spirit – Eph.1:17)
- <u>Righteousness</u> – forgiveness, justification
- <u>Sanctification</u> – cleansing, renewal, holiness
- <u>Redemption</u> – deliverance, freedom, restoration

Besides all the benefits of being a child of God that are noted in this chapter, write down others that come to mind, from your own experience, or from scriptures you know. This should amaze and bless you!

6 PAUL'S PURPOSE AND PASSION

1 Corinthians 1:17; 2:1-5; 4:1-21

By his own admission, Paul was not a great orator, nor educated in the world's wisdom. He confessed to fear, weakness and trembling when he preached the Word of God (2:1, 3 and 4). But he knew what his mandate was, and his lack of finesse or skill did not deter him from this. In fact, he suggests that fancy speech might even have detracted from the simplicity of his message (1:17). A carefully crafted sermon, delivered with eloquence, can be devoid of the Holy Spirit's anointing, or evidence of God's power to save, heal and deliver. It might impress people, but it does not change hearts. Paul's aim was not to please people, but to preach with power the full message of the Gospel entrusted to him!

Paul was certain of his purpose, and stated it in several ways, commensurate with the vastness of the task:

- To preach the Gospel (Good News) – 1:17
- To declare the testimony/mystery of God – 2:1
- To exalt Jesus Christ and His crucifixion – 1:17; 2:2
- To demonstrate the power of the Holy Spirit – 2:4
- To impart God's hidden wisdom/mystery – 2:6-7
- To teach what the Spirit had taught him – 2:12-13
- To be looked on as a servant of Christ – 4:1
- To be a faithful steward of God's truth – 4:1-2
- To warn and instruct as a loving father – 4:14-15
- To be an example worthy of imitation – 4:16-17

Paul knew that with such a heavy mandate on his life, he had to be daily living out the message he preached:

- He was <u>careful to live beyond reproach</u>, and not let the critics destroy his credibility or dissuade him from his purpose, knowing that not man, but God, is our judge (4:3-5), and we answer to Him only!
- He made it clear to the believers that there was <u>no competition</u> between him and the other apostles, to vie for the loyalty of the 'congregation' (4:6).
- He reminded them that <u>no one was better than another</u>; they could not boast in what they had - all their blessings were gifts from God (4:7-8).
- He and the other apostles were willing to be weak, debased, destitute and despised, even considered "*<u>fools for Christ's sake</u>*", in order to bring blessing to the Church (4:9-13).
- <u>He worked to support himself</u>, so as not to be a burden to the Churches (4:12; Acts 18:3; 20:34).
- Paul, as <u>their spiritual father</u>, took seriously all the implications of this, and promised to come shortly to help them work out their issues (4:18-21).

What lessons can you learn from Paul's life?

7 THE MYSTERY UNRAVELED

1 Corinthians 2: 6-16; 3:1-4

"Oh, the depth of the riches both of the wisdom and knowledge of God! How unsearchable His judgments and His ways past finding out!" (Rom.11:33)

Paul begins this short study by reiterating that he is not teaching the wisdom of man, which wisdom is fleeting, even as man is. He also suggests that God's wisdom can only be understood by mature believers (2:6). Later on, he reveals what he means by 'mature believers'.

Vs.7-8 — Little did Saul (later known as Paul) know, when Jesus confronted him on the Damascus road (Acts 9), the magnitude of the <u>Plan of Salvation</u> predetermined in God's mind before the world began, <u>to raise us to glory</u> (Heb.2:10). Prophets, priests and other writers of the Old Testament had hinted at the mystery of God's amazing wisdom (v.9; Isa.64:4; Psa.31:19). But no one, not even Saul, a devout and learned disciple of these writings, had been able to 'crack the code' of the mystery. So when God began to put His plan into action by visiting earth in human form, the ruling Roman governors unwittingly *"crucified the Lord of glory"* (v.8). *"Had they known they would not have"* been a part of the conspiracy to kill Jesus of Nazareth. How could they know that <u>He had to die</u>, in the torturous and inhuman manner they had devised, to be the sacrifice for the sin of all mankind?

Vs.10-13 — <u>The **key** to unraveling the mystery of God's plan is the Holy Spirit</u> (v.10-11). Before Jesus went to the cross, He promised His disciples that after He returned to heaven He would send His Spirit to live in them, and in all who would believe in Christ. He told them *"When He, the Spirit of truth, has come, He will guide you into all truth. . . and He will tell you things to come"* (John 16:13). The <u>only</u> way we can comprehend the things of God is if we have His Spirit living in us, *"that we might know the things that have been freely given to us by God"* through Jesus' death on the cross (v.12). We receive God's Spirit when we accept Jesus Christ as our Savior and Lord (Rom.8:9). <u>God's Spirit</u> within us <u>teaches our spirit</u> the wisdom of God's truths that our finite minds could never fathom! (v.13) <u>He is the conveyer of God's wisdom</u>!

In verses, 2:14-3:4, Paul groups people into **three categories**, based on our <u>ability to receive God's truth</u>:

1. <u>The **natural** man</u> (person) (2:14) – This person <u>has not received new life in the Spirit</u> by embracing salvation in Christ (John 3:16). He/she <u>has not been born again</u> by the Spirit into God's kingdom (John 3:3). Because he has not received the nature of God (2 Pet.1:4), he <u>is operating out of a sinful nature</u> (Eph.4:18-19). Nothing in him can relate to God's Spirit because he <u>is ruled by the law of sin and death</u> (Rom.8:2). So <u>the wisdom of God makes</u> no sense at all to him. It is like utter foolishness (1:18). Most people fit into this category!

2. <u>The **spiritual** man</u> (2:15-16) – This person has been <u>born again by God's Spirit</u>, so <u>has the nature of God</u>. Because God's Spirit lives in Him (Rom.8:11), he is <u>able to receive and understand the wisdom of God</u> which is spiritual. Our mind is renewed by the Word and the Holy Spirit (Tit.3:5) As Paul puts it here, *"we have the mind of Christ"* (v.16). A person who is truly spiritual is one who is <u>walking in righteousness</u>, <u>led by the Spirit</u>, <u>not fulfilling the desires of the flesh</u>, <u>quick to repent of sin</u>, and <u>following Christ wholly</u> (Phil.3:9; Rom.8:14; 1 John 1:9; 1 Pet.2:21).

3. The **carnal** man (3:1-4) – This is a person who has been born again, but <u>has not matured in his life in Christ</u>. Like a baby, he is unable to receive the solid spiritual truth of the Word (3:1-2 Heb.5:13-14). He still <u>clings to the things of the world</u>, and has not cleansed himself from attitudes and actions in his life that are displeasing to God. The <u>fruit of the Spirit is not evident</u> in him. As a result, there is envy, strife and division in the body of believers, and following men instead of Christ (3:3-4).

Why are some Christians carnal? 'Carnal' means fleshly (catering to what our flesh desires). A carnal Christian has not died to these desires (Rom.6:11-13; Eph.2:2-3). He has not yielded his body to the Spirit of God, or allowed the Holy Spirit and the Word of God to renew his mind (Gal.5:16; Rom.12:1-2; Eph.4:20-24). He still carries around the polluting corpse of the body of sin that died with Christ on the cross (Rom.6:6). Yuck!

If any of the previous paragraph describes you, you are probably quite miserable. The good news is, **you don't have to stay there!** Come to the Father, in repentance of carnality, coldness, contentions, etc. He will receive you, forgive you and restore you! Yield your life to the Holy Spirit. Relinquish the things of the flesh or the world that are not pleasing to God, and are keeping you from a close relationship with Him. Ask the Holy Spirit to reveal things within you from the past, that you have never resolved. There may be un-forgiveness, bitterness or resentment against others, or even yourself. Maybe you are filled with fear/anxiety, shame or guilt. God wants you be free of these crippling things. Jesus died to liberate you, to break the chains that bind you, and turn your mourning into joy! (Isa.61:1-3) Let Him do this, right now!

Spend time with God, in the Word and prayer, asking the Holy Spirit to guide you into His truth. As you learn and obey the truth, it will set you free (John 8:31-32). You will begin to grow into spiritual maturity, and to fulfill God's purpose for you. He loves you so much, and wants you to have His abundant life!

Which 'man' do you identify with? What are some clues of this in your life?

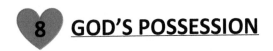

8 GOD'S POSSESSION

1 Cor.3:5-17; 6:12-20

One of the unique qualities of the Christian faith is that the Almighty God who created us does not wait for us to seek Him; He sought us! Jesus often used parables to teach the truths of God's kingdom, two of which focus on this amazing fact: "*The kingdom of heaven is like a merchant seeking beautiful pearls, who, when he had found one pearl of great price, went and sold all that he had and bought it* (Matt.13:45-46). The Church is that pearl, and Jesus paid the ultimate price, to redeem us out of the prison of darkness, to "*purify for Himself His own special people*" (Tit.2:14). We are HIS!

In another parable He says: "*The kingdom of heaven is like treasure hidden in a field, which a man found and hid; and for joy over it he goes and sells all that he has and buys that field*" (Matt.13:44). Paul, in our text, says:

"*You are God's Field*" – (1 Corinthians 3:5-9). Paul's main purpose is not to elaborate on the fact that as a Church, and as individuals, we belong to God, but that, like a field, we are to produce fruit for His kingdom. A field, if it is going to be fruitful, needs to be planted and watered. So, as God's ministers (v.5) and His fellow-workers (v.9; 2 Cor.6:1), Paul had labored to plant the Gospel seed at Corinth, and Apollos had faithfully watered the soil to nourish the growing seed. But God gave the increase. The Church is His field, and He brings forth the fruit!

Lest we are led to put all the onus for working in God's field on the appointed ministers and teachers, I want to clarify that as we grow and mature as believers, we need to realize that each one of us has a function in the Church (Rom.12:4-8). (We

38

will look into this later, as we study the twelfth chapter of 1 Corinthians.) For now, let us just consider a few points relative to our current text:

- Prior to planting the seed, the soil needs to tilled and softened by God's Spirit through <u>our prayers</u>.
- We are <u>all</u> called to <u>witness</u> – <u>planting the Word</u>.
- <u>We</u> can't 'convert' people to Christ. This is the work of the Spirit of God (John 6:44). <u>We</u> just <u>sow the seed</u>.
- Watering is done by <u>teaching the Word</u> and <u>building up believers in the Holy Spirit</u> (Tit.3:5; Eph.3:16).
- It is the life of <u>the Spirit</u> in us that <u>produces fruit and growth</u> – not our effort (Gal.5:22-23; John 15:4-5, 8)
- <u>We will be rewarded if we are faithful</u> to what God has called and gifted us to do (v.8).

In ch.3, v.9, Paul abruptly switches metaphors to bring out another important truth. *"**You are God's Building**"* - (1 Corinthians 3:9-15). <u>The architect is God</u>. He is the designer of <u>the Church corporately</u>, <u>and</u> of <u>individual believers</u>. In both cases, <u>we are God's building</u>. Paul was specifically chosen by God, in His grace, to be the wise master-builder who laid the foundation of the Gospel of Christ to build God's Church, of which <u>the foundation is Christ</u> (v.10-11; Acts 9:15). The prophet Isaiah wrote of this several hundred years before Jesus came to earth (Isa.28:16; 8:14; See Psa.118:22). Peter quotes these passages as he teaches on the same theme (1Pet.2:4-8).

<u>As a Church, and as individuals</u> we have built on the foundation of Christ and the Gospel of the cross. But, notice the warning in vs. 10-15. The warning is to those leaders that God subsequently gifted to the Church, to continue to build on this foundation with what is lasting, and beautiful in God's purpose for His Church. No doubt the "gold, silver and precious stones" include <u>sound doctrine and fidelity to the Truth</u>, as well as

operating in the power of the Holy Spirit. The substitute of any of these with a doctrine of works, adding to or subtracting from the truth, or twisting it to please people, and only operating in one's own power, constitutes wood, hay and straw, that will not pass the fire-test on the Day of judgment (2 Cor.5:10; Rom.14:12).

In reference to individuals, are we building our lives on the foundation of Christ and His Word, seeking His kingdom, and the things above, in order to become mature, Christ-like believers? Or are we carnal, worldly, and concerned only with what is temporary? (Vs.14-15)

Building on this metaphor (no pun intended), Paul once again segues into a new thought. Get ready – this one is mind-blowing! ***You are God's Temple*** – (1 Corinthians 3:16-17; 6:12-20). "And *the Spirit of God dwells in you*".

Paul reiterates this in his second letter to Corinth: "*You are the temple of the living God*" (2 Cor.6:16). Also see Rom.8:9-10. Because God's Spirit dwells in each one of us as believers, and since we all make up His Church, the Church is being built, believer by believer, into a place where God dwells, i.e. the house of God (Eph.2:19-22).

But once again, along with this amazing truth comes a warning. As Church 'watchmen', what and whom are we allowing into the Church that will defile it? See Matt.21:12-13; 2 Kings 23:4-7; 2 Cor.6:16a; 2 Tim.4:3-4; Rev.2:14-15; 20.

In 1 Cor.6:12-20, Paul addresses individual believers at Corinth with a stern admonition. I believe that now, more than ever before in history, we need to listen, and heed his warning! What are we allowing into our minds and bodies to defile this temple of God? (Rom.6:12-13, 12:2; Heb.12:15) Because we have been purchased by Jesus at great price, our bodies are not our own possession – they are to be for His purpose and glory. Is God honored by what I do <u>to</u> my body, or <u>with</u> my body (and mind), or what I feed them? Our God is a God of purity. My body and mind are His – made holy through His Spirit in me (v.17).

In light of this teaching, and of Paul's plea to believers in Rom.12:1-2, is it time to take stock of what <u>we</u> have in our homes and our churches, that defiles us instead of building us up in the truth? What do I listen to? What do I watch? What do I do in secret? Where do I spend my time, and with whom? Have I become so conformed to the world that the Spirit's voice is silenced? Do I need to do some serious repenting and 'house' cleaning??

 9 LESSONS ON STEWARDSHIP

1 Corinthians 4

As bearer of the Gospel of love and peace, Paul wanted people to see him and the other apostles not as haughty and unapproachable, or hiding behind any masks, but as:

- <u>Servants of Christ</u> (v.1), faithful and wise to serve, protect and provide for their Master's household (the Church) (Matt.24:45-46)
- <u>Ministers of the new covenant of grace in the Spirit</u> (2 Cor.3:6), in good conscience (2 Cor.4:1-2; 6:4), and in much patience during opposition and trials.
- <u>Faithful stewards of the mysteries of God</u> (vs.1-2; Col.1:25), to reveal to the Gentiles the mystery of *"Christ in you, the hope of glory"*, in all its bountiful riches and beauty (Col.1:27). The stewardship of this mystery was entrusted to Paul in particular – not to keep to himself, but to reveal, communicate, and expound on, in obedience, faithfulness and wisdom.

Paul knew that his call to the ministry was from God; and as a servant answers to his master, he was accountable to God, not merely to those he worked among (v.3). If we are leaders in the Church, God alone knows our hearts and can judge our motives for service. He is the One who rewards us according to our faithfulness in the task He has given us, and to our inner purity (vs.4-5). Are we, like Paul, able to testify in truth that we know of no fault in us that could be brought against us? And do we preach the whole truth of the Gospel, and only the truth?

In vs.6-21, Paul speaks to another issue, similar to the previous ones of sectarianism and carnality. There were displays of pride and arrogance among this body of believers (v.6). Paul reminds them that any spiritual gifts, blessings or knowledge that they had, were not to be boasted about, since they neither deserved nor earned them. They are all gifts of God's grace (v.7-8).

In contrast to some in the Church who were living like kings, and flaunting their riches, wisdom, prestige and might, Paul gives them a glimpse of what he and Apollos had endured because they had been faithful stewards of the Gospel of Christ (vs.6, 9-13). Like condemned criminals who were thrown to the lions to entertain the crowds in the Coliseum, their lives were constantly in danger (v.9). They were dishonored, ridiculed, counted as weak and as fools (vs.10, 13). They had endured thirst and hunger; they often wore rags and were beaten and homeless (v.11). They had to do manual labor in order to eat, and were persecuted and mocked, while blessing others and preaching the Gospel of love (v.12). (For a fuller, more detailed explanation of their hardships and suffering, look at 2 Cor.11:23-28. We can't comprehend the extent of what they endured for Christ!)

Why was Paul talking like this? He explains in vs.14-21 what is on his heart as he writes:

1. As a caring and, concerned father, he warns his *"beloved children"* against spiritual pride, not to shame them, but to exhort them (v.14).
2. He is not just one among many teachers. He had brought them to new birth through preaching the Gospel. They are his spiritual children (v.15).
3. He wants them to be walking in his ways, even as little children imitate their father. He is sending Timothy to them to remind them how they should be behaving as believers (vs.16-17).

4. He wants them to know that they are on a slippery slope, and they need to repent so he won't find it necessary to discipline them (v.21; Jas.4:6-10).
5. He assures them that he is indeed coming to them "*if the Lord wills*", and wants to come in love and a spirit of gentleness, not "*with a rod*" (vs.18, 21).
6. He reminds them that God's kingdom is never about man's boastful words, but demonstrates God's power to change lives (vs.19-20).

What are some things that God has given you, as a gift or responsibility that you need to steward faithfully? How is that going?

What things can get you off the track of conscientious and careful stewardship?

What have you learned from Paul's example in the way he was willing to be a servant, and be expended for the ones he was called to minister to?

10 IT JUST KEEPS GETTING WORSE!

1 Corinthians 5

As a backdrop to this chapter, please refer to the Introduction to this book, regarding the notoriety of the city of Corinth for the sensuality and prostitution in their pagan worship of Aphrodite/Venus, the goddess of licentious love (lust). In reference to the case to be addressed in this chapter, Paul says such behavior was taboo even among the pagans (v.1). So what happens when a situation like this arises in the Church? Paul makes several very strong points:

1. Sexual immorality/aberration is <u>not</u> to be either tolerated, accepted, ignored or sanctioned in the Church. It is certainly <u>not</u> an opportunity to brag about our tolerance (v.2, 6a).
2. Those guilty of such sin are to be confronted and judged, then removed from the fellowship so as not to desecrate the Church (vs.6-8, 13b). This discipline was sanctioned by Paul (v.3), who instructed the leaders to use his authority even in absentia. In the name and power of Jesus they were not to overlook the flagrant, unconfessed sin, but to remove the covering of the fellowship from the guilty one(s), allowing Satan to work in them the consequences of their sin, in order to bring them to <u>repentance, forgiveness and restoration to the fellowship</u> (vs.4-5; Gal.6:1). In 2 Cor.2:3-11, Paul shows that <u>forgiveness by the Church</u>, and <u>restoration in love</u> was his intent.
3. Until there was evidence of genuine repentance, the Church was not to fellowship with them (v.9). This applied not only to the sexually immoral, but included *"the covetous, idolaters, blasphemers, slanderers, drunkards or extortioners"* who called themselves believers. (v 11; 1 Tim.1:20) In vs.7-8 Paul uses the analogy of purging out the

old leaven at the feast of Passover, comparing the leaven to malice and wickedness, as opposed to unleavened sincerity and truth.

4. Note - In v.10 Paul clarifies that we are not to cut ourselves off from the people of the world who do all sorts of evil things. Rather we are to be salt and light to them (Phil.2:15; Matt.5:13-16). We are not the judges of those in the world (v.12-13).

Porn as opposed to Purity: The phrase 'sexual immorality' derives from the Greek words 'porne' and 'pornos', meaning 'to act the harlot, or to commit fornication/sex before marriage' (KJV). (Derivatives used in the original Greek translation also include adultery, unlawful lust (of either gender), incest, debauchery, whoremongering, prostitution, trafficking of people for sex exploitation, and even idolatry. I'm sure you have already recognized 'pornos' as the origin of the word 'pornography' (literally 'obscene paintings', which have been around for centuries in one form or another). In 1 Cor.10:5-8 and also in Rom.1:21-32 Paul describes the connection between idolatry and sexual depravity. It is not a pretty picture! Our generation/age does not have a corner on this degrading 'porn' market; media has just made it more blatant!

{It might be necessary to point out, as Jesus did, that it is just as wrong to think about doing these things as to take part in them (Matt.5:28). It is the pure in heart who will see God (Matt.5:8). Read Paul's strong words in Eph.5:3-7. Especially note verse four! Coarse, suggestive speech or crude jokes should never be heard from our lips! In Gal.5:16-25 Paul says that the key to a pure life is to walk in the Spirit. Psalm 119 emphasizes the importance of knowing the Word of God which keeps us pure (vs.1-3, 9). "Let us cleanse ourselves from all filthiness of the flesh and spirit, perfecting holiness in the fear of God". (2 Cor.7:1). "You are the temple of God"! (2 Cor.6:16)}

Leaders in the Church are like 'watchmen', who guard the gates to keep out what defiles. As the Bride of Christ, the Church is to be pure and holy (Eph.5:25-27). See Jesus' message to the Churches of Pergamos and Thyatira in Rev.2:14-16; 20-23.

How do you see the Church of today in comparison to the Corinthian Church in Paul's day, as to purity of life, and what is 'winked at'? Do you personally need to do some repenting and cleansing?

# 11 <u>MY RIGHTS!</u>

I Corinthians 6:1-11

Is it just me, or are there others out there who think that the number of incidences of suing and counter-suing is ridiculously out of control in our society today? What do you think of a believer suing another believer? Let's have a look at Paul's reaction to hearing that this was going on in the Corinthian Church. I hope that my paraphrase of his words will not min-imize the tone of sarcasm and disappointment in his rebuke:

1. How dare any of you sue a Christian brother in a worldly court, before an ungodly, and possibly corrupt judge, rather than deal with things <u>in the Church</u>, in a Christian manner? (vs.1, 4, 6)
2. Do you not realize that one day, as co-rulers with Christ, you will judge the world and fallen angels? (2 Pet.2:4) Isn't there even one person among you wise enough to settle your petty disputes? (vs.2, 3, 5)
3. Your actions are disgraceful. Shame on you! (v.5)
4. You have failed miserably to act in love. Rather than demanding your rights, causing undue loss to a brother, you should be willing to forgive, and accept loss and wrong against yourself (vs.7-8).

Paul is saying that as citizens of the Kingdom of God, we are no longer to live by the world's standards. We follow a new law of love, grace and mercy. We cannot name the name of Christ and continue to live under the control of Satan, the god of this age (2 Cor.4:4)

In vs.9-11 Paul further emphasizes this by reminding the Church that there are two dominions – the Kingdom of God, and the realm of Satan. The unrighteous ones listed in vs.9-10

live under Satan's dominion, and cannot inherit God's Kingdom
. . . unless . . . Take note of v.11: *"Such were some of you"*. Paul
had gone to Corinth with the Gospel message a few years earlier and remembers that some of the Christians he is writing to
were among those who were of that evil domain. . . *"But"* by
God's grace, the vilest of us sinners can be <u>washed from our sins</u>
by the blood of Jesus who died in our place. We are <u>sanctified</u>
(made pure and holy) by the work of the Holy Spirit and the
Word of God in us. And we are <u>justified</u> or declared righteous
before God by calling on the name of Jesus as our Savior.

We are totally forgiven of all past moral depravity and corruption. We are rescued from Satan's grip, and live a new life in
God's Kingdom of light, love, joy and peace. We become sons
of God and inherit all the abundant riches of His heavenly
Kingdom. What amazing grace!

Can you cite some examples of how a true believer acts, speaks
or thinks differently from the world's way?

12 TO MARRY OR NOT?

1 Corinthians 7

In this chapter, Paul writes on the matter of a godly marriage, and of purity in our lives, whether married or single. We don't know exactly what questions had come to Paul from the Church, but we can derive from his opening remarks (v.1-2), that they had to do with sexual misconduct. As a preface to his teaching here, let us be clear on a couple of points: Marriage was ordained by God from the start, when He said, about Adam, *"It is not good that man should be alone; I will make him a helper comparable to him"* i.e. Eve (Gen.2:18, 21-23). And God established His basic rule for marriage in v.24: *"A man shall leave his father and mother and be joined to his wife, and they shall become one flesh."* Having said this, we need to know that marriage is not the eleventh commandment, or a commandment at all; but rules of/for marriage are included in the Ten Commandments and marriage is protected by them. See Exod.20:14, 17.

Right out of the gate (v.2), Paul slams pre-marital sex as an option for believers , knowing that *"he who commits sexual immorality sins against his own body"*, which is *"the temple of the Holy Spirit"* (1 Cor.6:18-19). In light of this, if there is no self-control over their passion/lust, they are to marry (vs.2, 9). It is a well-known fact that sex with no commitment (i.e. out-side of marriage), brings a lot of heartache, hurt, disease and destruction to our lives. This is not in God's plan for His people!! God made the rules to protect us, not to deny us pleasure!

Vs. 3-6 contain some good insight into, and advice for, <u>a suc-cessful marriage.</u> The expression used by God of *"one flesh"* is the basis for Paul's instruction, that in order for both husband

and wife to be fulfilled, each has to meet the needs of the other, both emotionally (with love and respect), as well as sexually. Failure to do this, especially for any length of time, can result in one or both looking elsewhere for satisfaction, (leading to adultery and divorce).

The divorce debate comes up in vs.10-16. Usually, when both parties are totally committed to each other, to the marriage and to God, the idea of divorce does not even surface, let alone present as an option. But we all know that 'the perfect marriage' is not all that common. In the mind of God, marriage is a sacred covenant not to be broken, and Paul makes that clear in vs.10-11. On the other hand, should a spouse stay in a marriage where there is abuse, mental torment and danger of harm to one's self or to the children? I agree that marriage is sacred, and is a binding covenant, but I also believe that acts of violence, etc. can break the covenant, freeing the victim from the demands of the law concerning it.

Next (vs.12-16), Paul speaks to the issue of marriages where one spouse is a believer, and the other is not (an unequal yoke – 2 Cor.6:14). Paul takes the view that if the marriage is compatible/peaceful, and unless the unbelieving spouse wants to divorce, the believing spouse should not seek to end the union – for the sake of the children, and the witness to the spouse, perhaps bringing them to belief in Christ. What do you think?

Paul now seems to get off on a tangent, with the matter of circumcision and slavery (vs.17-24). But his purpose is to emphasize the point of the previous paragraph, that we are to stay in the marriage we were in at the time of becoming a believer. He sums up his argument in the words at the beginning and at the end of this section: *"As the Lord has called each one, so let him walk"* (v.17) and *"Let each one remain with God in that state/situation in which he was called"* (v.24).

This applies to marriage as much as it does to circumcision and slavery, (though not to ungodly lifestyles!)

As an unmarried man, Paul was not anti-marriage, but now argues that there are pros and cons for both camps. Speaking for himself, he had concluded it was probably best that he remain unmarried, considering the harsh living conditions and distresses he endured as a travelling missionary of that time in history. It was not a fitting lifestyle for a wife and family. Is he hinting in v.25 that God had given him the grace to live as a single man who could be trusted to live a pure moral life? I believe some are called to be single, and are quite content in this, as God gives them grace, and they find complete fulfill-ment in Him!

Briefly, from verses 26-35, we can learn: -

1. Not to be pressured by society to marry or remain single, but to act in the will and purpose of God.
2. Contrary to our dreams, marriage is not a breeze. Storms, struggles and troubles will come.
3. A married person's attention is focused on his/her spouse, with little time for the Lord.

There are different interpretations as to what Paul is referring to in the closing verses of this discussion on marriage (vs.37-38). Is he talking about a bachelor who can't decide whether or not to commit to marriage, but wonders (while she waits and gets older) if he can keep himself pure in a platonic relationship? Or is it about a father who lives in a culture of arranged marriages, and isn't ready to release his daughter into marriage with a man who may not treat her properly? Since we do not know what question he is answering, the answer may be ambiguous. In either case, to marry or not to marry is not the issue, as long as there is no sin involved.

In v.39 Paul interjects a law of the covenant of marriage, which gives hope to a widow who wants to remarry. The fact that her spouse has died means she is free from the covenant she made with him, and may remarry; the only stipulation is that she marry in the Lord (he must be a believer – 2 Cor.6:14). (The same law also applies to a lonely widower!) Even as Paul dutifully reminds the Church that remarriage can be all right, his final words, in v.40 reiterate his opinion expressed earlier in vs.7-8, that it really is better for them if they stay single, as he is! This makes me chuckle – I think he meant this sincerely, and it isn't a case of sour grapes!

Is there some of this teaching you disagree with? Which in particular, and why? Is your view scriptural?

13 CLASHING CULTURES

1 Corinthians 8; 10:14, 18-33; 11:1-16

It is common knowledge that whenever two or more cultures meet, toes are stepped on and people can be offended by the actions of others. Many of the believers at Corinth had come out of a culture of idolatry; others were Jews who had strict dietary rules, and observed a number of special feast days. Now, in Christ, they were delivered from idol worship and the restrictions of many ceremonial laws. However, a problem had arisen that affected both of these cultural groups. It had to do with eating meat which had been offered to idols.

In speaking to this issue, Paul reiterates that while we may think we have all the answers, and that what we believe is the only way to go, God is not impressed with our knowledge (v.1-2). Rather, it is our love for Him that gets His attention (8:3). **Knowledge** puffs us up in our own eyes; **love** builds up others (v.1). Therefore, love has to be the springboard for all our actions. Paul operates from this premise, and goes to great lengths to convince his readers to do likewise (v.7-13).

In case there was any doubt about the truth that there is only "*one God, the Father . . . and one Lord Jesus Christ*" (v.6), Paul emphasizes that it is this creator God whom we worship, and idols are nothing (v.4). (See Isa.44:9, 12-17). Other 'so-called gods' are merely the figments of man's imagination (v.5). There are thousands of such, worshipped in vain by millions all over the world!

While idols and other gods in themselves are 'nothing', worshipping them, i.e. idolatry, is strictly forbidden by God (Exod. 20:3-5, 32:6-8; 1 Cor.10:14). Our 'heart idols' are things that we cherish and worship more than God (Ezek.14:6-7). Even covetousness, and stubbornness are forms of idolatry, in disobedience and rebellion against God (Col.3:5; 1 Sam.15:23).

As we look at Paul's reasoning in both chapters eight and ten, we will observe some guidelines for dealing with controversial action, by living out the law of love:

- Give no offence to any in the Church (8:7-13; 10:32).
- Seek the good of others, not yourself (10:23, 24, 33).
- Eat what is set before you; ask no questions. Don't eat if you know it is defiled (10:18-22, 25-30).
- Do all to the glory of God (10:31).
- Don't judge others who abstain (Rom.14:1-13).

The case for head-covers and shorn locks is another cultural contention that surfaced at Corinth (ch.11:1-16). I wonder, in reference to Paul's remark in 11:2 about *"keeping the traditions"*, if head-covering is a carry-over from Jewish tradition, that he appears to be waffling on. There seems no such law from God about men praying with heads uncovered, or women not praying unless their heads are covered, or that a head-covering shows submission to authority *"because of the angels"* (v.10). Correct me if I'm wrong! (In some cases, head-coverings for women are still an issue of controversy, although not necessarily in church!)

And where does the Bible teach that even in nature, long hair dishonors a man, and that a woman should have long hair? (Vs.14-15) Do the statements in vs.8-10 not seem to be nullified by the words of vs.11-12? I guess (maybe as a contentious person), I agree with Paul's conclusion, that *"we have no such custom, nor do the Churches of God"*. Whew! What a relief! It is just not worth arguing over, even with yourself!

But, have a look at v.3, which I totally agree with. One reason is that this is corroborated by other scriptures, notably Gen.3:16b. It was a rule that came after the fall of man into sin, and possibly given as a protection for the woman (as her head, the man is her covering). The husband-wife relationship is a picture of Christ and the Church (Eph.5:22-33), and of the submission of Jesus to the Father (John 14:28). It is the God-given order, that works in the family and in the Church, for God's glory!

What are some modern-day examples of causing other believers to stumble by our actions?

In light of your answers, and of ch.10:23-24, what is the godly thing to do?

What problems might ensue if the wife assumes the role of 'head' in a family or if the husband does not?

14 RIGHTS AND REWARDS

1 Corinthians 9

In the first half of this chapter, Paul's pen explodes with rhetorical questions, reminding the Church of his right to remuneration for his labors among them as teacher, preacher of the Gospel and apostle of God.

His Credentials - vs.1-2

- He was a bona fide apostle (1 Tim.2:7).
- He was not a slave, but was born free (Acts 22:28).
- He had a special calling by Jesus (Acts 9:1-18).
- The Corinth believers proved his claims (vs.1-2).

His Lawful Rights – vs.3-6

- Physically – to have food and drink (v.4)
- Emotionally – the companionship of a wife (v.5)
- Financially – support from the Church (v.6)

His Arguments for These Rights – vs.7-14

- Soldiers are paid for their warfare (v.7).
- Farmers receive produce for their labor (v.7-8).
- Oxen eat the grain they are threshing (vs.9-10).
- The Levitical priests ate and lived off the gifts and offerings brought to the temple (v.13).
- Therefore, I (we) as preachers of the Gospel who sow to your spiritual needs, should reap material things from you in return (vs.11, 12, 14).

After clearly making his point with all this rhetoric, Paul comes out with a collection of conjunctions to bring us into the theme of the last half of the chapter - "But" (vs.15, 27), "For though" (v.19), "For if" (vs.16-17) and "Therefore" (v.26), predicated with "Nevertheless" in v.12. All this to explain that he was willing to forego all of the aforementioned rights, and how he viewed his calling. Perhaps you are thinking, "Was the man crazy?" Let's see if we can understand his reasoning.

First of all, Paul makes it clear that he has not demanded his rights in the past, and the arguments he has just presented are not a claim to these rights in the future (v.15). Perhaps we should be reminded here that Paul felt extremely indebted to Christ for his salvation, and for being entrusted with proclaiming the mysteries of the Gospel, not only to the Jews, but especially to the Gentiles (1 Tim.1:12-15). He considered this a most obligatory stewardship, which he dared not ignore. It was not the vocation he chose, but one that he was compelled to fulfill (vs.16-17). Because it was not his willing choice, he had no grounds for boasting, and he did not want to make it appear so by accepting money (v18). It was reward enough to see the fruit of his preaching in people's lives changed by his message (v.2; 1 Thes. 2:19). He did not want to hinder the Gospel by demanding payment for his preaching (v.12). To borrow the jargon of today, Paul was "paying it forward", as he exulted daily in the mercy and grace that had been so freely and liberally extended to him at a time when he was a violent enemy of Christ and of His followers.

Servanthood – vs.19-23: Paul's life was the epitome of servanthood, even though he was a free man. He was flexible, identifying with whatever group of people he was seeking to win to Christ. At the same time, he never compromised the truth, or his reputation as a minister of the Gospel and follower of Christ (v.21).

Paul's Ultimate Reward – vs.24-27: Paul reminds us that we are all in a race (Heb.12:1), and we must be disciplined (self-denial), and free of hindering weights. Whether we run or fight we need to be deliberate and not just play-act (which leads to disqualification). There is a prize waiting for all who run the race well and finish the course (This is not just for the missionaries and preachers!) (2 Tim.4:8, Jas.1:12) The reward of earthly gain meant nothing to Paul, but he longed to hear the words of his Master: "Well done, Paul, good and faithful servant! You have fought a good fight, and you have run a good race. Here is your crown; you have earned it." I can see Paul, not putting the crown on his head, but falling prostrate before the One he loved, and laying his crown at His feet. The crown was nothing compared to Jesus, and being with Him for all eternity. <u>He was Paul's Ultimate Reward!</u>

Comments: What do you make of this man, Paul?

15 RESISTING TEMPTATION

1 Corinthians 10:1-15

Although it is quite likely that the Corinthian Church was largely comprised of Gentiles, they had been led to Christ through Paul, a Jew. Paul taught them the mysteries of the Gospel of salvation by grace, through faith, as revealed to him by the Holy Spirit. He expounded to them from the Hebrew writings in the books of the law, history, psalms and prophets how it was God's plan to redeem a people for Himself out of all nations, through the sacrificial death of His Son. So it is no surprise that Paul uses the phrase *"our fathers"* (Israelites). He wants to make sure that as Gentiles they understand the history of Israel, and how it ties in with the Church. In vs.1-4 Paul refers to <u>experiences of Israel under the Old Covenant</u>, which <u>are a picture or foreshadowing/type of the Church under the New Covenant</u>. Implied here is that just as Israel was delivered from Egypt's bondage, so these Gentile believers were delivered from the old life of bondage and sin, and guided on a journey to a new life of freedom and blessing:

V.1 – Israel was led through the desert by a cloud that was a shield against the heat by day, and at night a fire that gave protection from predators (Exod.13:21-22). After the tabernacle was erected, the cloud settled over this place of worship, and continued to lead them along the way (Num.9:15-17). This fiery cloud looks ahead to the Holy Spirit who protects and guides us on our homeward pilgrimage (John 16:7, 13; Acts 1:8, 2:2-4).

V.1-2 – Passing through the Red Sea – representing water baptism – forsaking the old life for new life in Christ (Rom.6:4)

V.3 – Spiritual food (manna from heaven) – a picture of Jesus, the Bread of Life from heaven, whose body was broken to give us life and health (Matt.26:26, Isa 53:5).

V.4 – Spiritual drink (water from the rock) – Jesus, the Water of Life, whose body, like the rock, was cleft. His life-blood flowed out to cleanse us from the defilement of sin, and to infuse us with His own eternal life, thus establishing the New Covenant (Matt.26:27-28). This is also representative of the unending blessings of Christ and the gifts of the Holy Spirit (John 7:37-39).

In spite of Israel's miraculous deliverance from Egypt, and God's care, provision and protection on their way to Canaan, *"with most of them God was not pleased, and their bodies were scattered in the wilderness"* (v.5). They became examples for us of what NOT to do! (vs.6, 11). Paul gives a stern warning against four things that they fell into because of the lust (wrong fleshly desires) in their hearts. Obviously he recognized this as a very real problem in the Church at Corinth as well!

V.7 – idolatry – lusting after other gods (Exod.32:1-6) V.8 – sexual sin – lusting for other women (Num.25:1)

V.9 – testing Christ – lust for unclean meat (Psa.106:28)

V.10 – complaining – lust for the old life (Deut.1:27)

NOTE - The result in each case was sickness, death and destruction. May God fill us with holy desires for Him!

In v.12, Paul warns against placing confidence in prior good behavior as a weapon against falling into sin. We are to be diligently on guard at all times, against all kinds of temptation. He reminds us in v.13 that temptations are the norm – other people face similar temptations all the time! AND, temptation is not sin. It comes to us as a thought, from our old enemy, the devil (who often uses people to deliver his messages!) It only becomes a sin when we listen to it, entertain it in our thinking and let our own fleshly desires draw us to it until we give in to its enticement (Jas.1:13-16). The key is to resist it at its first appearance, and nip it in the bud by shutting it out of our mind ("*bringing every thought into captivity to the obedience of Christ*" - 2 Cor.10:5). God has provided us with His Spirit, and with weapons to fight against the wiles of the devil (Eph.6:10-18; 2 Cor.10:3-5). God, in His faithfulness will not allow temptation to be more than we can deal with; He enables us to escape and come through victorious over it. That's good news! (v.13)

Do you see a connection between 'lust' as we have seen it in this chapter, and the tenth commandment, "You shall not covet"? Are they the same?

What do you think is the antidote to coveting?

16 ❤ THE LORD'S TABLE

1 Corinthians 11:17-34; 10:16-17

As Jesus shared the Passover meal with His disciples just before His death by crucifixion, He put into place a ceremony that represented His death as a sacrifice for sin. His command was that we keep on performing the simple yet profound act, until He comes back again, as a continuing reminder of what He was willing to do to redeem us. It is known in various circles by different names – Holy Communion, Eucharist, the Sacraments and the Lord's Table. There is one label that I am prone to think is a misnomer. 'The Lord's Supper' likely comes from the fact that it was instituted on the occasion of 'The Last Supper'. Jesus was observing the Passover Feast with His disciples – a meal of roasted lamb, eggs, bitter herbs, vegetables and unleavened bread, etc. to remember the eve of Israel's escape from Egypt under Moses' leadership.

However, the only two items Jesus gave to His friends, to represent the elements of the New Covenant, were a shared piece of <u>bread</u> (after blessing it) and a cup of <u>wine</u> (*after* the supper - 1 Cor.11:23-26). I believe Paul is emphasizing my point in 11:20, where he is saying, *"When you come together (as a Church – v.18) in one place, it is <u>not</u> to eat the Lord's Supper"*. It was precisely because they mistakenly considered it and called it a 'supper' that confusion had erupted among the Church members. It is not a pretty picture, as Paul describes it in vs. 17-22 and 33-34. More on this later!

I am of the opinion that this celebration of the Lord's death was never meant to be a 'supper' or a meal by any other name. Paul goes on, in vs.23-26 to relay to the Church the short message Christ had given him – such a profound concept imbedded in a few simple statements and represented by only two ordinary emblems. Jesus Himself did not give this institution a name; He gave Paul just a short meaningful statement to share with the Church, of the <u>New Covenant</u> that had been <u>cut with His very life-blood</u>, of <u>His body broken for our healing</u>, <u>the promise of His coming again</u>, and <u>two simple elements to remind us of His death</u>, and <u>to proclaim it to others</u>.

In ch.10, vs.16-17 Paul refers to the wine as the <u>'cup</u> of blessing', and the communion/fellowship/sharing of the <u>blood of Christ</u>. The <u>bread</u> is the communion, etc. of the <u>body of Christ</u>. As the body of Christ (one body) we all share of that one bread i.e. the body of Christ. As I was pondering how to write about this beautiful subject, God distinctly directed me to <u>verse five of Isaiah fifty-three</u>. This verse from the Old Testament opened my eyes to the truth of the New Covenant. It sums up in four concise statements the reason for celebrating 'Communion' in the Church. I hope it will bless you!

"***He was wounded for our transgressions***" The wounds from the crown of thorns, plus the nails and spear that pierced his hands, feet and side, caused the life-blood to flow from Him. "*It is the blood that makes atonement for the soul*" (Lev.17:11). "*Without shedding of blood there is no remission/forgiveness*" of sin (Heb.9:22).

"***He was bruised for our iniquity***" As Jesus hung on the cross, "*<u>the LORD laid on Him the iniquity of us all</u>*" (Isa.53:6). Iniquity refers to the sins inherent in the generations. It was the compounded weight of all the iniquity in every person from Adam forward, in every generation past, present and future, that crushed and bruised His body. "*<u>He made Him who knew no sin to be sin for us</u>, that we might become the righteousness of God in Him*" (2 Cor.5:21). The horrific impact of this on the pure and undefiled Son of God, cannot be imagined – no doubt it crushed His spotless soul as well as His body. Jesus took the curse of sin upon Himself, <u>so we could be free from generational curses and the disease and sickness that sin's curse brings on mankind</u>. What amazing love!

"*The chastisement for our peace was upon Him*" "*When we were enemies, we were reconciled to God through the death of His Son*" (Rom.5:10). Jesus took the punishment for our sin, so we could have <u>peace *with* God, and the peace *of* God</u>. This is how much God loved us – that "*He Himself bore our sins in His (Jesus') own body on the tree*" (1Pet.2:24), so He could bring us into His family as dear, beloved children.

"<u>*By His stripes we are healed*</u>" Throughout His earthly life, and especially as He approached the cross, Jesus endured grief, sorrow, rejection, shame, affliction, pain and loss (Isa.53:3, 4, 7). He bore <u>our</u> griefs in order that we can be healed from all the hurts, shame and guilt in our body, soul and spirit.

At this point, I want to take you back to 1 Cor.11:27-32, to examine the connection of the Lord's Table of Communion with the last statement in Isa.53:5, <u>and</u> the prophecy concerning Jesus Christ, in Isa.61:1-3. I have always been puzzled by the words "*unworthily*" (KJV)/ "*in an unworthy manner.*" See 1 Cor.11:27, 29. The common explanation focuses on the unworthiness of the partaker, <u>not</u> on the manner of the action as being unworthy. The <u>Greek word used</u> here is anaxios, and is pronounced (an-ax'-ee-ose), <u>meaning 'irreverently'</u>, (as opposed to an-ax-ee'-oss, meaning 'unworthily'). (Note the difference in accent and final vowel sound). Looking again at the context, (vs.17-22, 33-34), we know why Paul used this word. The action of the believers in the Corinth Church was decidedly irreverent, to say the least. To Paul, it was despicable and shameful (v.22). Also, because of their misuse and mis-understanding of this sacred and meaningful ceremony that

65

was designed to unify them in one Body, factions and divisions had arisen among them (vs.18-19). The problem addressed was not WHO was partaking of the Lord's Table, but HOW they were celebrating it.

So what shall we say about the usual preamble to this event? I am not suggesting that the Table of the Lord is for everyone present at Church. But I do take exception to the emphasis on examining ourselves to determine <u>if we are worthy</u>. Who are we to judge worthiness? Is any one of us worthy? Really! Neither the person partaking nor the one serving the elements can be the judge of the heart. More to the point, <u>"Am I doing this reverently and with understanding of its meaning?"</u>

This brings us to another puzzling question I have had, which is tied to the previous one. (I really do not like an unsolved puzzle!) What does <u>*"not discerning the Lord's body"*</u> mean, and why does it cause <u>weakness, sickness and death</u>? (vs.29-30) Notice that Paul does not mention a lack of discernment of the Lord's blood. Simply put, most believers *do* 'discern' <u>His blood,</u> recognizing that Jesus' blood was spilt for the forgiveness of their sin; and they accept this forgiveness. But many who name the name of Christ have not <u>ever</u> discerned <u>His body,</u> which was not only bruised for our generational iniquities, but *"carried our sickness and pains"* (Isa.53:3-4; Matt.8:17). Since Jesus bore our pain in His body, we are healed by His stripes (repeated cruel lashing with barbed whips) (1 Pet.2:24). He bore that pain, so that we could be free of pain. He became weak so we can be strong. It was the torment He endured, that enables us to live free of the affliction of all kinds of infirmity and disease.

When Jesus called out *"IT IS FINISHED!"* on the cross, it was a cry of victory over sin, death and the enemy, and over all the consequences of sin in our lives. Why was Jesus constantly healing people while he lived on earth? (Luke 4:18-19; Acts 10:38) It is because He knew sickness was the work of the devil, and contrary to what many believe, He really does want us to be well. This includes emotional and mental healing. Jesus was subjected to shame, to free us from shame. He bore the guilt of our sin, to free us from guilt. He came *"to heal the broken-hearted"*, to *"proclaim liberty to the captives"*, *"to comfort all who mourn"* and to *"give the garment of praise for the spirit of heaviness"* (Isa.61:1-3; 3 John 2).

It follows that if we do not discern this amazing truth about the body of Jesus, we are neglecting, even negating one-half of the Gospel of Salvation. We are not crediting His bruising or His stripes as worthy of our belief for healing in our life. This is *"not discerning the Lord's body"*. *"For this reason"* i.e. because we do not believe, the result is: (You guessed it) *"many are weak and sick among you, and many sleep"*/die prematurely (vs.30). It is as easy for God, and as much His desire to heal us, as it is to forgive our sins. We accept the life-blood of Jesus to give us new life in our spirit; why do we not accept the bread of life to nourish, strengthen and heal our bodies from the ravishes of sin? Just as we receive forgiveness, so we can receive our healing – by believing the truth, and receiving it as ours by faith!

To close, I hereby unofficially declare Isa.53 (Key verse – 5) to be the "love chapter" of the Old Testament, connecting it to the New Covenant of Grace and Peace established by the shed blood and broken body of Jesus Christ, Son of God and Son of man. And I name Isa.61:1-3 "the proclamation of the Gospel of Christ", as true for us today as it was for the first believers!

The next time you take Communion, thank Jesus for His blood, shed for the forgiveness of your sin. And thank Him for His body, bruised for your healing. Thank Him for your healing, as you receive it in faith!

17 IGNORANCE IS ~~NOT~~ BLISS

1 Corinthians 12

"Now concerning spiritual gifts, I do not want you to be ignorant" (v.1). Paul's concern for the Corinth believers led him to write these words and this chapter under the direction of the Holy Spirit. As I write, over 2,000 years later, I share this concern for the Church of today, and echo his words. I dare say we, too, have worshiped idols of one sort or another at one time or another (v.2). Now, as with the Corinthian believers, the Holy Spirit has given us birth into God's kingdom, and adoption into God's family, enabling us to call Jesus our Lord. If we do not call Jesus 'Lord', we do not know the Holy Spirit (v.3).

In vs.4-6, Paul briefly mentions gifts of the Godhead to the corporate Church and to individuals: manifestation gifts to individuals from the Holy Spirit; ministry/office gifts from Jesus, for the Church leadership (Eph.4:7-16); and activity gifts from the Father to believers, to build up and serve the body (Rom.12:3-8). His main focus here is the gifts of the Holy Spirit, to introduce the theme that is forefront in chapters 12-14.

One Spirit, Nine Gifts (vs.7-12) These Gifts of the Holy Spirit manifest as supernatural abilities in individual believers who are yielded to Him. They are the Gifts of:

- Revelation – wisdom, knowledge, discerning spirits
- Power – faith, healing, miracles
- Utterance – prophecy, tongues, interpreting tongues

The gifts of the Holy Spirit are given for specific needs and in specific situations to show His power and to bring people to faith in Christ. They are given to believers at the will of the Holy

Spirit (v.11). Paul emphasizes that they are all from the Holy Spirit, and are to be used to minister to others (vs.7-10).

My concern and question is: Why is the Holy Spirit not giving these gifts to God's people in many Churches today? I certainly believe He still wants to manifest His wisdom, miracles and revelation in the Church through His people (Eph.1:17-19). *Why wouldn't He?* He wants us to be able to discern spirits, so we can deliver people from the oppression of the enemy, Satan (1 John 4:1; Luke 10:17-19). *That's why Jesus died!* It is His desire to heal people and perform great miracles through us (Matt.10:8; John 14:12). *This brings glory to Him!* And He loves it when we pray to Him and prophesy in tongues (Mark 16:17-18). *It's His language after all!*

These gifts of the Holy Spirit are available to His Church! He wants us to operate in these gifts, for the building up of the Church (edifying the believers). I suggest several reasons why many Churches function as if there were no Holy Spirit:

- A woeful lack of teaching in the Church on the work and gifting of the Holy Spirit
- A pervasive unscriptural/erroneous belief that the Holy Spirit no longer works through these gifts (*He does where He is acknowledged!*)
- The hardness and unbelief of our hearts
- Our self-sufficiency, our materialism, and our idol- filled lives which quench and grieve the Holy Spirit, so He cannot work in us
- A teaching of work-based, self-focused, non - Spirit-led 'Christianity'
- An unwillingness to repent of sin in our lives, and a lack of desire to live wholeheartedly for God.

One Body (vs.12-31)

Throughout the New Testament, the Church is known as the body of Christ, who is its Head. To introduce this topic, Paul mentions the greatest manifestation of the Holy Spirit of all – baptizing us into this body, and filling us with His presence (v.13). Quite humorously, he uses this analogy of a body to explain that no one member can function apart from the other members of the body; nor are we to exalt our position or function in the body over that of another. There must be no schism or division in the body (lest we end up with a spiritual auto-immune disease, where we bite and devour one another to the point of self-consumption! [Gal.5:15]) We each have a function, and 'checking-out' is not healthy for the body or for the individual who leaves.

Just in case we might think we are all doing our own thing, independent of each other or of God, in v.28 Paul lists three <u>office gifts</u> appointed by Christ to the Church - apostles, prophets and teachers; two <u>activity gifts</u> from the Father - helps and administration; and for re-emphasis, the <u>manifestation gifts</u> of miracles, healings and tongues from the Holy Spirit. All are important!

In many Churches there seems to be a willingness to let the office gifts from Christ operate in the Church. And of course, to deal with all the needs and programs and activities, the volunteer base must consist of people of various Father-endowed gifting and abilities. But does the Church really need the <u>manifestation</u> gifts? After all, "We have survived for hundreds of years without them. What's the big deal, anyway?" Let me suggest a few things to think about:

Paul appears to give more 'press' to the Holy Spirit gifts than to the others. He certainly does not minimize their importance to the Church, or infer at any time that they would become unnecessary or be revoked. He warns us <u>not to</u> "*quench the*

Spirit", but to walk in the Spirit, in His power and gifts. Stephen said "*You always resist the Holy Spirit*" (Acts 7:51). As I think more about it, I wonder if we are afraid to let God be God, afraid that the Holy Spirit will do supernatural and strange things that are way out of our comfort zone. It comes down to this: Do I care so much about what people will think should the Holy Spirit manifest in and through me, that I am not willing to yield myself to Him and "*earnestly desire the best gifts*"? (v.31)

Are you ready to ask God for the filling and baptism of the Holy Spirit, and to yield completely to Him, so He can give you His gift(s) as He sees fit, to manifest His power in and through you?

18 "A MORE EXCELLENT WAY"

1 Corinthians 13

When Paul introduces this chapter with the words "A *More Excellent Way*" in ch.12:31b, he is not only defining love; he is describing God's love, which should manifest in and through us to others in the way He loves. In vs.1-3 he emphasizes the absolute necessity of love in all that we do, but especially in the operation of the gifts of the Spirit (ch.12). No matter how gifted we are in tongues or prophecy or working of miracles, unless we love those who hear the words we speak and witness the miracles, it is just discordant noise. If words of wisdom, knowledge or discernment are not spoken from a heart of pure love, they are worthless. While faith without works is dead (Jas.2:17), faith apart from love is pointless and useless. Even the gift of generous giving and martyrdom must be based on love if it is to have any merit.

Read vs.4-8a, substituting the word "love" with the word "God", to get a picture of the purity, sincerity and endurance of God's love. This is the love He loves us with! (It might be helpful here to compare different translations, for the various descriptions of what love does or doesn't do). Read the same verses again, using the word "Jesus" in place of "love". As you do, think about this: This is the kind of love He wants us to display/portray through His Spirit in us. After all, it is the Holy Spirit who pours this love into our hearts, as we read in Rom.5:5. We must receive it and walk in it!

The third time through, as you read these same words, substitute 'I' or your name for 'love'. Ask yourself: "Does this describe my love for others? Or has the pure love of God in me been crowded out by negative and damaging emotions from the old nature? Is my 'love' a self-centered, judgmental, and rude love, which is not love at all, but just an empty, hollow and hypocritical façade?"

Vs.8-12 remind us that while we are here on earth we will not be perfect in all the Spirit's gifts, because of our sinful flesh; and with the perfection of heaven, when we are face to face with Christ, these gifts will become redundant, and will cease. However, faith, hope and love will endure forever, with love being the greatest of all attributes. Therefore, "*PURSUE LOVE*" (14:1a).

Why will the gifts of the Spirit be unnecessary when we get to heaven? (Refer back to the previous chapter to review why they were given).

Do you believe that we would be more effective in both ministry and evangelism if we operated in the gifts of the Spirit? Why/Why not?

19 A DESIRABLE DESIRE

1 Corinthians 14:1, 3, 5, 24-26, 29-40

"*Desire spiritual gifts*" These opening words sound almost like an imperative, an order, a command – even more so as we examine the meaning of the Greek word 'zeloo' (dzay-low'-oh): "to be zealous for, to burn with desire, to pursue ardently, to desire eagerly or intensely". Does our interest in receiving these gifts come anywhere close to this level of desperation to have them? It seems quite obvious that the Apostle Paul was enormously convinced of their importance in the Church i.e. in the lives of the believers (even a Church filled with strife, division and selfishness; or more realistically, especially such a Church!) No doubt, and correctly so, he knew the difference that would be evident if all the believers operated in the gifts of the Holy Spirit, in love! This is sort of hinted at when he says to "*especially desire the gift of prophecy*" (v.1, 5, 39). (Note that this is not foretelling the future, but a word from the Holy Spirit to speak to a person's need)

As we see in v.3, the gift of prophecy, used in love, does three things to build up the Church (vs.4b, 22b):

1. It edifies the people to whom it is spoken; (and it strengthens their faith and builds them up in it).
2. It exhorts/encourages believers to faithfully live a life of hope and purity.
3. It comforts and gives hope to those who are going through difficult situations.

As has already been noted, prophecy is usually spoken to believers, for the benefit of the Body (the Church). But it is also a sign to the unbeliever, who, amazed at the words spoken through the Holy Spirit, revealing some unknown fact about a person, realizes this is from God, (vs.24-25), and is led to faith in Christ.

One reason Paul zeroes in on the gift of prophecy is to give some guidelines to the Church at Corinth, to deal with the issue of confusion that had come with 'everyone talking at once'. (This may have stemmed from the fact that there was no resident pastor there, who would do most of the preaching). He has no problem with them all wanting to share some truth (v.26), but insists there must be an established order, so that people are able to hear, and be edified (vs.26b, 33, 40). The basic rule is to regulate the number who can share, one at a time, and the others should assess the message given, as to the <u>criteria for prophecy</u>: Does it edify, exhort or comfort? Does it line up with scripture? (Vs.29-32).

In the middle of the confusion cited in v.33, and the order of v.40, are a couple of hard-to-understand verses about women speaking in Churches (vs.34-35). A very thorough examination of the original Greek text by a present day scholar, Jonathan Welton, revealed that this passage is in quotation marks, indicating that Paul is quoting from the letter the Corinthian Church had previously written to him. It seems that they had been making up rules in his absence. His somewhat sarcastic words in vs.36-38 tell me that Paul did not agree with them or take ownership of this teaching.

More to the point is the issue of godly order, with God the Father being head over Jesus the Son, who is head of the man, who in turn is head of the wife. It addresses the matter of aggressive wives with passive husbands, which can cause confusion in the family as well as in the Church, when women usurp the place of authority designed for the husband. In humility and love, let us each seek the Lord as to our role, in the home as well as in the Church (Eph.5:22-33). Note the words of v.31a "You can all prophesy". Sister, that includes you and me! (This was prophesied in Joel 2:28-29!)

Getting past the problems addressed, I hope that you will desire the gifts of the Spirit. If you do, prepare your heart before God, through repentance and prayer, to be open to receive and operate in one or more of the gifts the Holy Spirit wants you to have. Ask Him! And don't be surprised if one day you see something happen that is 'out of this world', that will amaze you, and everyone around you! You will be humbled, blessed, thankful and exhilarated, because you have been a vessel used by God to edify, heal or help someone God put in your path for that express purpose! And He will be glorified!

"*Therefore . . . desire earnestly to prophesy*" (v.40).

20 OUT OF CONTROL

1 Corinthians 14:1-23, 27-28

The other problem that had come up at Corinth had to do with another Spiritual gift – speaking in tongues. Once again, it wasn't that they weren't using the gift, but that they didn't quite understand how and where it should be used. It was 'out of control', which is odd, because in the best meaning of its usage, as <u>our tongue is controlled by the Holy Spirit </u>in us, it truly is <u>out of our control</u>. In fact, Paul likens it to being under the influence of wine, where we don't know what we are saying (Eph.5:18), and often, neither do those who are listening! I love the way Paul, referring to the Spiritual gift of tongues (1 Cor.12:10) puts it in v.2 of ch.14: "*he who speaks in a tongue does not speak to men but to God, for no one under-stands him; however, in the spirit he speaks mysteries*." Wow! That intrigues me, and makes me want this special gift!

Now I realize, as we broach this subject, that you may be among those who have chosen to "throw out the baby with the bath water". This saddens me, because not only are you missing out on <u>this</u> gift, but perhaps on <u>all </u>of the supernatural gifts of the Spirit (ch.12:7-11), that are ours, as part of our inheritance in Christ. Speaking specifically about tongues, since that is the focus of this chapter, Paul <u>nowhere</u> says that we should not speak in tongues, that this practice is wrong, or to be disdained/rejected. Quite the opposite. He often emphasized throughout his writings that <u>speaking in tongues is important, vital and useful to all believers</u>!

The Importance of Tongues to Paul:

<u>V.4</u> – *"He who speaks in a tongue edifies himself"* (cp. Jude 20: *"building yourselves up on your most holy faith, praying in the Holy Spirit"*).

<u>V.5a</u> – *"I wish you all spoke with tongues".*

<u>Vs.14-15</u> – *"If I pray in a tongue, my spirit prays, but my understanding is unfruitful". "I will pray with the spirit"* . . . *"I will sing with the spirit".* . .

<u>V.18</u> – *"I thank my God I speak with tongues more than you all".*

<u>V.39</u> – *"Do not forbid to speak with tongues".*

<u>Eph.6:18</u> – *"Praying always with all prayer and supplication in the Spirit"*

<u>Phil.3:3</u> – *"We . . . worship God in the Spirit".* (Compare John 4:24: *"God is Spirit, and those who worship Him must worship Him in spirit and in truth"*).

Just for clarification, the 'tongues' mentioned in this chapter, elsewhere in the New Testament, and in the Church, are referred to variantly as 'unknown tongues' (strange languages), 'the Spirit language', 'a spiritual language', 'other tongues', 'new tongues' or simply 'speaking in tongues'. See Acts 2:4; 10:46; 19:6; Mark 16:17. A tongue is a language of the Holy Spirit (one of many), which He speaks out of <u>our</u> spirit, where He resides, to help us intercede, praise and grow in faith.

The History and Purpose of the Gift of Tongues

We first encounter tongues in the book of Acts, when, as <u>a sign/evidence of the baptism by the Holy Spirit</u> on the ten dozen Jews gathered in the upper room, *"they were all filled with the Holy Spirit and began to speak with other tongues, as <u>the Spirit gave them utterance</u>"* (Acts 2:4). In this instance, the tongues were understood by the crowd of people (Jews) from every country and every language in the then-known world (Acts 2:5-11).

Later, Peter was sent to the house of Cornelius, the Gentile centurion, to proclaim the Gospel to him. As he and his household received the Word which Peter preached, *"the Holy Spirit fell on all those who heard the Word"* (Acts 10:44). This time, as a sign to the Jews that *"the gift of the Holy Spirit had been poured out on the Gentiles also . . . they heard them speak with tongues and glorify God"*. (v.46).

Still later, Paul came to Ephesus and found some of John the Baptist's disciples who had not heard of the Holy Spirit; but after they were water-baptized in the name of Jesus, *"when Paul had laid his hands on them, the Holy Spirit came upon them, and they spoke with tongues and prophesied" (Acts 19:6).*

We don't see the 'tongues' evidence every time a person is saved, and receives the <u>Holy Spirit</u>. But, when we pray for and receive His <u>baptism</u>, or <u>anointing for ministry</u>, we are given this gift, which we may choose to use or refuse, as with any gift. May we recognize its value in our life!

We conclude from these accounts that one reason for speaking in tongues was as evidence of the baptism of the Holy Spirit. A second purpose of the gift of tongues from the Holy Spirit, is <u>to build oneself up in the Lord, and in faith</u> (1 Cor.14:4; Jude 20).

Thus it is given <u>for private use to communicate with God</u>, and <u>receive revelation</u> from Him (1 Cor.14:2, 15).

Thirdly, praying in the Spirit (in tongues) <u>enables the Holy Spirit to intercede for us and through us</u> when we don't know how we should pray in a given situation (1 Cor.14:14; Eph.6:18). We don't have to search for words, to try and express what we cannot, *"but the Spirit Himself makes intercession for us with groanings which cannot be uttered . . . He who searches the hearts knows what the mind of the Spirit is, because He makes intercession for the saints according to the will of God"* (Rom.8:26-27).

Tongues becomes <u>an amazing avenue of praise</u>, when our speaking turns to singing in tongues, in the Spirit. (1 Cor.14:15). Eph.5:18b-20 describes it so beautifully, as *"speaking to one another in psalms and hymns and spiritual songs, singing and making melody <u>in your heart</u> to the Lord, giving thanks always for all things to God the Father, in the name of our Lord Jesus Christ"* When a group of believers, large or small, sings in tongues, the sound is breath-taking. It is like the most exquisite, fine-tuned symphony of instruments, blended in perfect harmony under the direction of the Holy Spirit, and rising like the sweetest perfume in praise to the Father and the Son. Awesomely, incredibly indescribable!!!

Some Guidelines for the Gift of Tongues

Although speaking in tongues is for the purpose of edifying believers, and is ideal for private prayer and worship, it is not limited to this. It can also be practiced by all, in a group of believers, by mutual agreement, <u>if</u> there are no unbelievers present (1 Cor.14:23). Where unbelievers are present, it should not be practiced <u>unless</u> there is someone there to interpret the meaning /message. Also only two or three should speak, in turn, each one followed by the interpretation (vs.13-17, 19, 27-28, 33). Then it is a sign to unbelievers (v.22). In vs.6-21, the point is made by Paul that believers come together for mutual edification, which means that others will not be edified by the speaking in tongues, unless it is interpreted. This is why prophecy should supersede tongues as a practice in Church, along with words of revelation and knowledge, as well as teaching (14:6).

We need to remember that the gifts of the Spirit are not to be sought after for the sake of the gift, or the honor of having the gift, but for the benefit of others in the Church, and ultimately for God's glory and fulfillment of His Divine purpose in and through us.

Which of the nine manifestation gifts of the Spirit do you desire? Why? How can you receive it (them)?

21 WHAT IF???

1 Corinthians 15:1-9, 29-34

In the opening words of the fifteenth chapter of this Corinthian letter, Paul confirms that he had brought the Gospel to Corinth, having received it by revelation from Christ, and that the Corinthians addressed in this letter had received his message and believed in Christ. By their enduring faith, they proved they were truly saved. Theirs was a heart commitment to follow Christ and not just a mental assent to His teaching (vs.1-2). In vs.3-4, Paul sums up the Gospel message: the death of Christ for our sins, His burial and His resurrection on the third day. All of this had been foretold in the Old Testament scriptures. His crucifixion was described in Isa.53:5, 12, His burial in Isa.53:9, and His resurrection in Psa.16:10. What makes Jesus unique among the 'leaders of religions', is that He rose from the dead. Because this was not normal, Paul corroborates it by recounting several post-resurrection appearances of Jesus, before He ascended to the Father (vs.5-7).

In vs.8-10 Paul marvels at the grace of God in his life. God not only forgave him for persecuting the early believers, and gloriously save him, but He chose him to be His special Apostle to the Gentiles. In gratitude to God for His amazing grace, Paul expended himself far more than any of the other apostles (by God's enablement). It did not matter to him whether it was he or another apostle who preached the Gospel; what was important is that the Corinthians had believed! (v.11)

Much to Paul's chagrin, apparently some people in the Corinth Church were denying or refuting the teaching of the resurrection of the dead (v.12). This is a much more serious issue than any Paul has had to deal with up until now in his letter.

Resurrection is so foundational and vital to Christianity that Paul attacks the problem from several angles. (It may appear in vs.13-19 that he is using circular reasoning to prove his point!)

In these verses, and vs.29-32, with each statement building on the prior one, Paul looks at the hypothetical 'IF' of the matter. Let's follow with him to his conclusion.

<u>If there is no resurrection from the dead</u>:

- Then Christ could not have risen (v.13),
- So then the message of the Gospel is empty (v.14),
- Therefore our faith in God is pointless (v.14),
- Which would mean that all the apostles are false witnesses by preaching the resurrection (vs.14-15).
- If there is no resurrection, Christ did not rise (v.16),
- Therefore our faith in Christ is worthless (v.17),
- We are still in our sins (v.17),
- Believers who have died are forever lost (v.18),
- There is only hope in Christ in this life (v.19),
- So we are more to be pitied than any other (v.19);
- The sacrament of baptism has no meaning (v.29). "*We were buried with Him through baptism into death, that just as Christ was raised from the dead by the glory of the Father, even so we also should walk in newness of life*" (Rom.6:4). If there is no resurrection from the dead, why be baptized?
- So why were Paul and his fellow-missionaries risking their lives for the Gospel on a daily basis, if death is the end of everything? (v.30-32)

Paul closes his argument with a warning (v.33-34), saying in effect, "Don't be deceived by these false teachers who tell you there is no resurrection. Stay away from them! Wake up to life in righteousness in Christ – don't be led astray. You should know better than to walk in ignorance when you have been taught from God the truth of the resurrection".

Why is the truth of resurrection of the dead such a vital tenet of the Christian faith?

Apart from the resurrection of Christ, what makes resurrection unique to the Christian faith?

Why does the resurrection give you hope?

22 THE FINAL VICTORY

1 Corinthians 15:20-28; 35-58

"But" – When you see or hear this word, you can expect a shift in thinking. In this case, it signifies what Paul knew beyond any shadow of doubt: Christ rose from the dead! He had met Him when Jesus talked to him from heaven on the Damascus road. (Acts 9:3-6) Later, he was caught up to heaven and received amazing teaching and startling revelations from the mouth of Jesus (2 Cor. 12:4). In spite of all arguments to the contrary, Paul knew that <u>Jesus is alive</u>; and because of this, he himself would one day rise from the grave (vs.20, 24). As Paul explains, just as the first piece of fruit on the vine is a promise of the coming harvest, in the same way the resurrection of Jesus is a promise of <u>our</u> resurrection.

Anticipating the questions of what our resurrection will be like (v.35), Paul uses metaphors from the natural or earthly to explain the truth of the spiritual or heavenly. He brings out several universal principles:

- When a seed is sown in the ground, the body/shell of the seed dies, and new life springs up from the germ within that seed (v.36) So, too, when our body decays, the life within (i.e. the spirit) brings forth new life.
- The new plant initially feeds on the flesh of the old seed to form a new body (vs.37-38). In a similar way, our soul does not die, but is changed and rises as part of our new glorified body.
- God has given every seed a distinct body, whatever body he chooses. The seed of men, animals, fish and birds have different kinds of bodies (vs.38-39).

- God has created other bodies with physical life but not soul life, such as all kinds of plants (Gen.1:12).
- Heavenly bodies (sun, moon, stars) do not have life, but each has its unique glory. Terrestrial bodies such as rocks and water also have their own particular beauty (vs.40-41).

All this to make the point that just as God has given a special body to each part of His original creation, so for His new creation (2 Cor.5:17), He will give us the special resurrection body of His choice. The characteristics of this resurrected body are contrasted with those of our current bodies (vs.42-49):

The Old Body	The New Body
Subject to corruption	Incorruptible (vs.42, 53)
Subject to death	Immortal (vs.53-54)
Without honor/dignity	Glorious (v.43)
Natural, physical, earthly	Spiritual (vs.44-45)
Earthy (dust)	Heavenly (vs.47-48)
In Adam's image	In Christ's image (v.49)
Dead through Adam	Alive in Christ (vs.21-23)

Why a new body? *"Flesh and blood cannot inherit the kingdom of God; nor corruption inherit incorruption"* (v.50). However, as is obvious, "we can only imagine" what our new bodies will actually be like! I am all right with the surprise element! Frankly, I can't imagine!

How and When will the Resurrection Happen?

- In a moment, in the twinkling of an eye - v.52
- When the last trumpet sounds - v.52
- Dead believers will rise to eternal life - v.52
- Living believers will join them in the air - 1 Thes.4:17
- Both the dead and the living will be changed and clothed with new, incorruptible bodies –v.52-53

This mass resurrection of every believer of all ages in a split second will no doubt be the most awe-inspiring, spectacular and supernatural event of world-wide scope in the history of mankind. I simply cannot wrap my mind around what an impact this will have on the spectators, who realize they have been "left behind", or the cosmic chaos it will cause. For those *"caught up in the clouds to meet the Lord in the air"*, it will be a thundering <u>victory celebration</u>, reverberating like the sound of millions of heavenly choirs throughout the universe, which has been groaning for millennia in anticipation of that day. It is a <u>proclamation of freedom</u>, when *"creation itself will be delivered from the bondage of corruption into the glorious liberty of the children of God"* (Rom.8:19-23)!

As Paul puts it, in a quote from Isa.25:8 and Hos.13:14, *"Death and hell are swallowed up in victory"* (vs.54-55). Through the death and resurrection of Christ, we will be resurrected, with <u>victory over</u> the <u>sin</u> that came through Adam, and was revealed by the law; <u>over death</u> that came as a result of sin, and <u>over hell</u> that awaits the unbeliever. They will no longer have any power over us! (Vs.56-57) ***"Thanks be to God"***!

The upshot of all this is that *"we shall always be with the Lord"* (1 Thes.4:17). Wherever He is, we will be. This includes reigning with Him as kings and priests during the millennium (Rev.20:4). He will reign until He has put all enemies under His feet (1 Cor.15:25-27). He will then deliver the kingdom to God the Father, and He too will be subject to the Father, *"that God may be all in all"*.

(It is to be noted that Paul does not teach here about the judgment seat of Christ. However, this is a subject he deals with in the book of 2 Corinthians – fuel for a future study!)

To wrap up this teaching of Christ's return for the saints, he exhorts the Corinth believers, along with us, to *"be steadfast, immovable, always abounding in the work of the Lord, knowing that your labor is not in vain in the Lord"* (v.58).

The words that come to me at this point are, *"How, then, should we live"*? If you knew Jesus was returning in the next few days, or even tonight, what would you do so you would *"not be ashamed before Him at His coming"* (1 Jn.2:28)? How about if you had a month's warning? Are you ready?

 23 WITH LOVE, PAUL

1 Corinthians 16

As you read through the final chapter of Paul's letter, jot down some things that indicate his care and concern for the Church (not just at Corinth, and not just collectively, but for individuals and fellow-workers). Be prepared to share with your study group.

How were the believers at Corinth to treat the missionaries that Paul sent to help them? (See vs.10-11; 15-16; 17-18.)

What verses in this chapter bring out the 'love' theme?

Are you convinced that Paul lived out the message of the 'love chapter', based on this letter he wrote to deal with so many problems? Can you give some examples from previous chapters?

"*And now abide <u>faith</u>, <u>hope</u>, <u>love</u>, these three; but **the greatest of these is love**.*" Do you agree with this? Why?

SEGUE

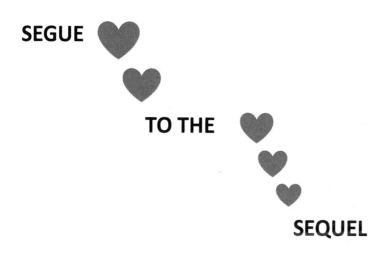

TO THE

SEQUEL

<u>We have all seen or experienced it</u> - a child falls, and runs sobbing to his/her mother with a bruised hand, elbow or knee, and 'Mommy kisses it better'. The child's sobbing stops, and play resumes. Somehow the love portrayed in the mother's soothing words, and in the touch of her lips, erases the hurt and the 'owie' goes away.

We have seen from the previous study that the cross is the theme of Paul's love-message to the Corinthian Church. It is the cross of Jesus that takes the 'owie' out of life, and has rescued us from the fear of death (John 10:10; Heb.2:14-15). This is why He had to die!

When you first saw the title of this book, did you see the word 'ouch'? Unless you happen to be color-blind, you probably didn't, because the cross changes 'ouch' to 'touch'. The love of the Father portrayed in the cross heals hurts and restores us to wholeness, in body, soul and spirit. Like a mother's kiss, the truth from the mouth of Jesus erases what is wrong in our lives, as we receive this healing and restoring touch of His love!

You may have guessed by now that some of my favorite scriptures are found in the 'Gospel' of Isaiah in the Old Testament. It is such 'Good News', full of the message of God's love and the amazing exchanged life He wants to give us. The following words about Jesus are so beautiful that I will not try to simplify them, but just let them touch you as they have touched me, with life-altering healing, deliverance and freedom:

> *"He was wounded for our transgressions,*
> *He was bruised for our iniquities;*
> *The chastisement for our peace was upon Him,*
> *And by His stripes we are healed."* (Isa.53:5)

"The LORD has anointed Me to preach good tidings to the poor; He has sent me to heal the broken-hearted, to proclaim liberty to the captives, and the opening of the prison to those who are bound . . . to comfort all who mourn . . . to give them beauty for ashes, the oil of joy for mourning, the garment of praise for the spirit of heaviness; that they may be called trees of righteousness, the planting of the Lord, that He may be glorified" (Isa.61:1-3). What indescribable love!!

Unless you have read the book we know as Second Corinthians, you may be asking, "So, how did it turn out? Was there a great awakening in the Church? Were the problems solved, and 'they all lived happily ever after'?" Well, not so much. While some things had been resolved, certain destructive influences from outside had come in. Paul made a painful return visit and then wrote a severe letter to deal with these matters. The book we are about to study is probably Paul's final letter to the Church there, and we can sense in his words the disappointment he felt in these people who were dear to his heart. If everything was as Paul desired, we might not have had a sequel to the story, which contains some of the information we have noted.

In 2 Tim.3:16-17 we are reminded that *"All Scripture is given by inspiration of God, and is **profitable for** doctrine, for reproof, for correction, for instruction in righteousness, that the man (or woman) of God may be complete, thoroughly equipped for every good work."* And as we open the pages of Paul's second letter to the Corinthians, which is a part of the canon of Scripture, we are in for a smorgasbord of all of these foods for the soul, some more palatable than others perhaps, but all necessary and wholesome. Let us come with a healthy hunger and thirst so we will be nourished and *"strengthened with might through His Spirit in the inner man"* (Eph.3:16). Are you ready?

I   HOW DID HE DO IT?

2 Corinthians 1: 1-11; 4:8-18; 11:23-27

The familiar and signature salutation in v.1 confirms that Paul, called by God to be an apostle of Jesus Christ, is the one who pens this lengthy letter. And, as in his first letter to the Church at Corinth, he includes other saints in his readership. Even to this day, his message is relevant to us, the Church of God, wherever or whoever we are, because it is the eternal truth of God that he proclaims – the message of "_grace to you and peace from God our Father and the Lord Jesus Christ_" (1:1-2).

(V.3) - Before launching into the first of three records of his extreme hardships as an apostle, Paul gives praise to God for His <u>mercy</u>, and <u>comfort</u> in all the suffering. He was experiencing the promise of God in Isa.66:13: "_As one whom his mother comforts, so I will comfort you._" And Jesus, just before His death, promised His grieving disciples that the Father would send His Spirit to them to be their comforter, helper and advocate (John 14:16-18; 15:26; 16:7-13). By extension, this is also a reality for believers today. God the Holy Spirit is our 'in-house' security system against the enemy's intrusion!

Paul understood the concept of 'paying it forward'. With every increasing tribulation, God's encouragement had multiplied to him, so he could help the persecuted believers to realize that God would not only enable them to endure the trials, but also console them and deliver them from the afflictions of the enemy (2 Cor.1:4-7).

How was Paul able to endure suffering for Christ? After Jesus had accosted him near Damascus (Acts 9), Paul had three days,

97

with eyes blinded, and without food or drink, to contemplate what had happened to him. He knew he had encountered the living Messiah and was changed forever, brought from darkness into light. He recognized God's great love, mercy and grace in revealing to him the truth that Jesus is the Son of God, Messiah, who by His ignominious death and His resurrection had rescued him from an even greater death. So even as he frequently faced the sentence of physical death, he believed that God would deliver him (2 Cor.1:8-10). He also knew the believers were praying for him, so he would be kept alive to continue bringing the gift of Life to many (v.11).

Paul was intensely sorrowful over his pre-conversion zeal as a Pharisee, that led him to persecute Jesus' followers (Phil.3:5-6). But his zeal was redirected, and it seems at times that he was not only willing to suffer as he had caused others to suffer, but to revel in his suffering, if it meant identifying with Christ, and manifesting Jesus' life in his body (1 Cor.4:10-12). Also, at the outset, God had told him through Ananias, *"I will show him how many things he must suffer for My name's sake"* (Acts 9:15-16), so he 'knew it was coming', though not what form it would take! But, by God's grace, he was "hard-pressed on every side, yet not crushed; perplexed, but not in despair; persecuted, but not forsaken; struck down, but not destroyed" (2 Cor.4:8-9). He did not give up, because he knew the *light sufferings of this fleeting life* could not be compared to the *weight of the eternal glory* that would be his (v.13-18; Rom.8:18). It is worth it all!

As part of the proof of his apostolic credentials, here, in chapter 11, Paul gets into the specifics of what he suffered simply because he followed and served Christ. The list in vs.23-25 is not easy to read; and it is difficult to imagine how a person could endure all this and still be alive, let alone even more committed to Christ and dedicated to God's calling on his life. It is hard to fathom how men created in God's image could inflict such cruel punishment on a fellow human being. Such vile hatred against Christ-followers is spawned in the mind of Satan himself. He infuses his lies and venom against Jesus into the hearts of men, who become his agents of destruction against those who worship God, as he once did.

We don't have to look farther than our media screens to know that hundreds and thousands of people of all ages, and from many countries are facing such atrocities and worse, as I write. Those who try to escape the horror face the perils listed in vs.26-27. What does one do in light of this unconscionable evil and barbarity? If the apostle Paul when facing persecution, and Jesus when facing the cruel cross needed prayer support, how can we not hold up these precious innocent ones before God, for sustaining grace and courage, for protection and safety, for provision and peace, even as many look death in the eye many times over before ultimate martyrdom?

What would I do if I were facing extreme persecution because of my faith? Would God's grace be sufficient???

II A TRANSPARENT LIFE

2 Corinthians 1:12-2:17; 7:2-16

Unlike the Pharisees of New Testament times, whom Jesus labelled 'hypocrites', Paul, transformed Pharisee with an indisputable pedigree, could confidently attest that his conscience was clear concerning his conduct among his fellow men. He was transparently sincere, and without duplicity. His godliness was authentic. He did not depend on man's wisdom, but walked in the grace of God, especially in his ministry to the Church at Corinth (1:12). In this letter he is not trying to impress them with some new teaching, but is reviewing and expounding on truth he had already taught them. He was hoping they would grasp the Gospel in its fullness, and that at the return of Christ, they would be able to 'brag on' him, and he on them (1:13-14).

In 1:15-19, 23-24 and 2:1-4, he shares that he had planned to bless them earlier with a visit, on his journey to Macedonia, hoping they would help him on his way. He did not do this, but could testify before God that he was not reneging on his promise, but simply did not want to come to them in displeasure over their unrepentance. He loved them dearly, and did not want to cause them more sorrow, but to give them more time to work out the sin issues, so that there might be mutual joy at their reunion. Having preached Christ among them in God's anointing, he was confident that the Holy Spirit would work in them to be obedient, and the rift between them could be healed. (1:20-22).

Ch.2:12-13 - Another reason for Paul not visiting Corinth sooner was the vision he received from God while in Troas, in which God redirected him to Macedonia (v.12; Acts 16:8-10).

Feeling the urgency of this call, Paul left for Macedonia in spite of his concern that he hadn't met up with Titus (No I-phones back then!). Are we flexible and obedient when God steps in to change our plans?

Godly Sorrow and Repentance - 2 Cor.7:2-12. The problem Paul referred to in the previous discussion was the shocking incident of immorality in the Church (1 Cor.5), that was ignored and tolerated with seemingly no sense of shame. In Paul's last letter to them he called the Church on it, instructing them to deliver the guilty party to Satan, in order that he might receive the due consequences in his body, to hopefully bring him to repentance and restoration. Until then, they were not to have any fellowship with him, so as not to defile the Church. It appears the Corinthians did as Paul had instructed, and the ostracized man had truly repented and changed his life-style. Somewhere between his writing of ch.2:13 and of 7:6, Paul had found Titus, who told him how the Church had sorrowed over Paul's letter of admonition. It was a godly sorrow, which led to their repentance of wrong, and resulted in a clearing of the innocent, a concern and alarm that such evil could have been among them, and a longing and desire to deal with the issue of concern. Paul was delighted to hear this news, and that they appreciated Paul's love and care for them. He was thankful that their sorrow was not excessive, and did not cause undue guilt or regret. They felt no offence towards Paul or Titus (7:13-16).

The Healing of Forgiveness – 2 Cor.2:5-11- However, Paul is grieved that the Church was still holding the wrong against the person they had disciplined. His says they are to forgive the man, and to comfort him, so he isn't overwhelmed with sorrow caused by blame and guilt. They are to reaffirm him with their love, and restore him back to their fellowship. They had passed the obedience test of Paul's letter, but now they needed to obey him in forgiveness, since Paul had already forgiven him, as an example of Christ's grace (2:5-10).

The primary reason for forgiving (in all instances), is "*lest Satan should take advantage of us; for we are not ignorant of his devices*" (v.11). The word 'forgiveness' is God's concept, and it is vital for us, His children. Under Satan's tutelage, un-forgiveness in our heart will escalate to resentment, retaliation, anger, bitterness, hatred, violence and murder unless we repent of it and receive God's forgiveness. As we release to God the one who hurt us, we are freed. If we do not forgive, we "drink poison and expect the other person to die". Do yourself a favor - Don't become hard and bitter – FORGIVE!

2:14 - Paul injects a sudden praise-phrase to God, "*who always leads us in triumph in Christ, and through us diffuses the fragrance of His knowledge in every place*". He re-phrases the statement he made in Rom.8:37 – "*In all these things we are more than conquerors through Him who loved us*". In spite of all the attacks of the enemy, the victory is ours in Christ! Paul gave all the glory to God for using him as the 'perfume atomizer' through whom the Gospel permeated and affected people's lives. Some, repulsed by the fragrance of the Christ, continued on the pathway to eternal death, but others were drawn to Christ and received abundant eternal life (vs.15-16).

V.17 – Paul could honestly say that he did not, like some, compromise the pure message of the Gospel for gain. His motives were sincere and his life was an open book before God, whom he gladly served as a humble and faithful ambassador.

Are there some things in my life that may indicate a somewhat less-than-transparent life before God and others? I can hide things from people, but God knows all my thoughts, motives, and attitudes (Heb.4:12-13). *"Search me, O God, and know my heart . . . and lead me in the Way everlasting."* (Psa.139:23-24).

Is the fact that many people will not receive the Gospel message a valid excuse for not proclaiming it by our lives and words? Why?

How can the way we live affect how our message will be received by people we witness to?

III THE LETTER OR THE SPIRIT?

1 Corinthians 3

In this letter Paul does a lot of 'speaking in his own defense', and in defense of the other apostles, which we will address later. Here, he introduces a vital truth by referring to the custom of letters of recommendation sent from a Church where a pastor (or a Church member) has been, to the Church where they are now going to be ministering (or attending) (v.1). Paul says he does not need a letter of approval – the transformed lives of the believers at Corinth proved he was for real, and what he preached to them was the truth. Everyone could see that they had changed, because the Holy Spirit had written the truth of Christ in their hearts (v.2-3). Similarly, they were like a letter written by Christ on Paul's heart, and were very dear to him.

Vs.4-6 - Paul knew by experience that the miraculous change in his own life had nothing to do with his own goodness or effort in keeping the law; it was God, the Holy Spirit, who had given him new life in Christ, and enabled him to be an effective conveyor of this truth to the world. This message was not about keeping the law, because in reality the letter of the law is a message that condemns. It shows us our sin, but can never forgive our sins or justify us before God (Rom.3:20). Paul came to preach the "new covenant", cut in blood by Jesus, Son of God, when He died on the cross, and ratified when He rose from the dead (Mark 14:24). All we have to do is receive His gift of life! (Rom.6:23; John 3:16)

In vs.6-18, Paul contrasts the old covenant of 'the letter of the law' with the new covenant of grace. He does not say the law is bad. The law, being from God, was perfect – too perfect for us to measure up to – a stopgap until it was time to introduce the new covenant (Gal.4:4-5).

LAW - Old Covenant	GRACE - New Covenant
- Ministry of death -7	- Ministry of the Spirit – 8
- (The letter kills) – 6	- (The Spirit gives life) - 6
- Engraved on stones - 7	- Written on the heart – 3
- Was glorious – 7, 10	- Is exceedingly glorious - 9
- Had passing glory – 7	- Has remaining glory – 11
- Condemned us – 9 -	- Makes us righteous – 9
- Its glory was veiled – 13	- Reveals God's glory – 18
- Blinded the mind – 14	- Transforms the mind – 18
- Darkened the heart – 15	- Enlightens the heart – 17
- Led to bondage – 17	- Brings liberty – 12, 17
- No access to God - 18	- Full access to God – 18

"*Through Christ Jesus the law of the Spirit of life set me free from the law of sin and death. For what the law was powerless to do in that it was weakened by the sinful nature, God did by sending His own Son in the likeness of sinful men to be a sin offering. And so He condemned sin in sinful man, in order that the righteous requirements of the law might be fully met in us, who do not live according to the sinful nature but according to the Spirit*" (Rom.8:2-4 NIV). **"Jesus has become a surety of a better covenant'**!! (Heb.7:22)

Am I living under the bondage of the law, or in the freedom of grace, led by the Holy Spirit? (Gal.3:3)

IV   TREASURE IN CLAY POTS

2 Corinthians 4:1-7

"Therefore. . .", refers back to the exultant declaration of <u>the glory of the New Covenant</u>, which <u>causes Paul to declare</u>, in thankfulness that he has been entrusted by God with such an awesome ministry of proclaiming this message; and because he has received abundant mercy, <u>that he will not lose heart</u>/ become discouraged due to opposition. He is filled with such a passion for the Truth that <u>he determines to continue his commitment</u> to:

- Renounce secret shameful thoughts and deeds
- Use no sort of deception, trickery or crafty slyness
- Not distort, corrupt or dilute the truth of God's word
- Display the truth clearly in word, deed and demeanor
- Walk before God so as to give no offence to anyone

Paul esteemed the Gospel message to be a priceless and beautiful treasure, to be handled with the utmost care so as to protect its purity. It is a message that changes lives, because it is the Gospel of God – Father, Son and Holy Spirit. If it is altered, it becomes ineffective. It is not the messenger, but the truth of the Gospel that convicts sinners of their sin, and need of a Savior. The Holy Spirit draws sinners to Christ, who is the Truth that shows the Way to Life, and to the Father's love. Through Christ's sacrificial death in our place, the Father can forgive us, clean us up and place us in His family. And He has a staggeringly, outrageously bountiful inheritance for us, a taste of which we experience here as we walk with Him!

God unveils the glory of His Gospel of the New Covenant to all who will respond to the Spirit's call. To those who will not come, it is veiled; they cannot understand or appreciate its glory. Satan, our arch-enemy, has blinded their eyes; he knows that if they could see the beauty of the Gospel they would believe, and so be delivered from Satan's kingdom into the kingdom of God (vs.3-4).

May nothing we do or say <u>ever</u> diminish the worth of the Gospel in the eyes of anyone! It is the light of the glory of God manifested through Jesus, the image of God. He is the One we preach, as bondservants of Christ. The telling of the Gospel must never exalt <u>us.</u> This Gospel is the light that God commanded to shine out of darkness; to shine on us, and in our hearts; to open our eyes to the Truth, so that we could know the beauty of God's glory as we gaze on the light of Christ's face (vs.5-6).

Why does God put this priceless treasure of His glory light in our frail bodies? (v.7) Is it because He wants to shine out from us to all we meet, with the love, joy, peace, kindness and gentleness of His blessed Spirit? The intensity of His glory is diminished by our outer casing, but His light shines out clear and steady as long as we do not hide it with the grime of our grouchiness or greed, etc. or allow hidden sin to sever the connection to God, the powerful source of the excellence. Let us protect and share this treasure of glory light! See Matt.5:14-16.

V PREPARED

2 Corinthians 5:1-11

Knowing at least in part the difficult life Paul lived, in his ministry as an Apostle two thousand years ago, it is small wonder that he often thought of dying, and faced it many times. It's not that he was afraid to die. On the contrary, he considered death gain, and to be with Christ much to be desired (Phil.1:21-24). He expresses assurance here in our text, that even if the tent we dwell in (our body) is destroyed by abuse at the hands of evil men, or by disease or starvation, it is of no concern or consequence. After all it is just where we live, and like all houses, decay and weathering happen. We are not a body with a soul; "we <u>are</u> a spirit, we <u>have</u> a soul, and we <u>live in</u> a body". The body is temporary! The soul and spirit live on.

When we are ready to die and leave our 'shell' behind, our mortal body is replaced by a new, indestructible <u>house</u> for our soul and spirit, in heaven, <u>prepared by God</u>, which will endure for all eternity (v.1). We long with a groaning ache for that new body (vs.2-4). Not only does God have <u>a body prepared for us</u>, He is <u>preparing us for that body</u>. As the guarantee of this, He has given us His very own Spirit to live in these mortal bodies. No wonder we long for our heavenly home! (v.5) This is why we walk by faith instead of by sight (v.7). Things we cannot see are far more real than what our eyes behold. As long as we are at home in our mortal bodies we are absent from the Lord, and we would much rather shake off this old building to be with the Lord. This gives us hope! (v.6)

In vs.9-11, Paul reminds us of something else we need to be <u>prepared for</u>. It is to be our aim to live a life that is well-pleasing to God, because as believers, we will all *"appear before <u>the judgment seat of Christ</u>, that each one may receive the things done in the body, according to what he has done, whether good or bad."* 1 John 2:28 exhorts us *"And now . . . abide in Him, that when He appears, we may have confidence and not be ashamed before Him at His coming"*. Will He say *"You have been a good and faithful servant"*?

Paul adds, in v.11, *"Knowing, therefore, the terror of the Lord, we persuade men; but we are well known to God"*. (The question here is not how well I know God, but does He know me as His child?)

Am I prepared to die, and am I looking expectantly for the coming of Christ, and being with Him in heaven?

Am I living a life pleasing to God, so I will be prepared to face Christ at His judgment seat?

What will I do to be prepared, and not be ashamed as I stand before His searching gaze?

VI COMPELLED BY LOVE

2 Corinthians 5:12-7:1

A song by The Mills Bros. (1954), says "The whole town's talking about 'The Jones Boy', He acts mighty peculiar now . . . He just isn't the same somehow . . . He hops, he jumps so merrily over the water pumps . . . The buzz is over the fences that he's going out of his senses . . . But I just happen to be the Jones boy, and I happen to be in love." What is it about love that makes us do crazy things?

By Paul's own admission, sometimes he was thinking "I must be out of my mind!" In this letter, he makes several comments about acting or talking like a fool (11:16, 21, 23: 12:6, 11). His excuse? You guessed it! LOVE – for God, for Christ, for the believers. In the second verse of this study, (5:13), he says, "*If we are out of our mind it is <u>for the sake of God</u>*"; I Cor.4:10: "*We are fools <u>for Christ's sake</u>*"; 2 Cor.11:1-2: "*bear with me in a little folly . . . for I am jealous <u>for you</u> with a godly jealousy*".

<u>Compelled to Live for Christ</u> - "*The love of Christ compels us*" (5:14). The ultimate love is giving your life for another. Jesus did this and more, taking away our sins, and rising again to give us new Spirit-life, with a divine nature (v.15-17; 2 Pet.1:4). Our old nature was crucified with Christ, and we are called to live this new life for Him, in the power of His Spirit (the power that raised Jesus from the dead). How can we ignore His love, and live for ourselves? Have old things really passed away? <u>We are not our own. We have been bought at a tremendous price</u> (1 Cor.6:19-20).

<u>Compelled to be Ambassadors</u> – 5:18-6:10 – "*Now then, we are ambassadors for Christ*" (5:20). Let's look at this topic by

drawing parallels between the qualifications and expectations of an earthly ambassador and those of an ambassador of heaven on earth. An ambassador:

- Is a citizen of the sending kingdom, not of the host country. *"Our citizenship is in heaven"* (Phil.3:20).
- Is appointed by the ruler of the sending country. Jesus said *"I chose you and appointed you that you should go and bear fruit"* (John 15:16).
- Is an official representative of his country. *"You shall be witnesses to me to the end of the earth"* (Acts 1:8).
- Has the authority of his government behind him. *"He (Jesus) gave them power and authority over all demons and to cure diseases"* (Luke 9:1).
- Serves his country and fellow-citizens with excellence, and is a good steward. *"As stewards of the mysteries of Christ . . . be found faithful"* (1 Cor.4:1-2).
- Has an assignment. *"<u>God has given us the ministry of reconciliation . . . and has committed to us the word of reconciliation</u>" - "<u>Be reconciled to God</u>"* (5:18-6:2). *"Go into all the world and preach the gospel"* (Mark 16:15).
- Does not get involved with local affairs. *"Set your mind on things above, not . . . on the earth* (Col.3:2).
- Does not bring dishonor to his home country. *"Give no offense in anything . . . as ministers of God"* (6:3-10).
- Uses his country's resources to protect himself and his fellow citizens from harm *"by the word of truth, the power of God, the armor of righteousness"*. (6:7)
- Keeps in touch with home base. *"Let your requests be made known to God* (Phil.4:6). *"Pray"* (1 Thes.5:17).

<u>Compelled to Pursue Holiness</u> - 6:11-7:1 – Paul's heart seems to be hurting deeply as he admonishes the Church for not being completely honest with him, as he has bared his soul to them. He pleads with them as a father to his children, to

111

own up to what he obviously already knows. It almost sounds like a community conspiracy to keep the secret, whatever it was. If we look at the next few verses, we might assume it had something to do with alliances with non-believers, such as in marriage. His argument is, that as a child of God, in fellowship with a holy God, there can be no union with the world; no communion between:

RIGHTEOUSNESS	and	~~LAWLESSNESS~~
LIGHT	and	~~DARKNESS~~
CHRIST	and	~~BELIAL~~
BELIEVER	and	~~UNBELIEVER~~
TEMPLE OF GOD	and	~~IDOLS~~

"You are the temple of the living God". Therefore, *"Come out from among them and be separate" says the Lord. "Do not touch what is unclean, and I will receive you. I will be a Father to you, and you shall be my sons and daughters." "Therefore, having these promises, beloved, let us cleanse ourselves from all filthiness of the flesh and of the spirit, perfecting holiness in the fear of God"* (6:16; 7:1). Amen!

Do I 'cheat on' God, by flirting with the world? By harboring idols in my heart? By defiling myself with what I see and hear? By ungodly associations? By not spending time with Him? By not worshipping and praising Him? May His love compel me to pursue holiness!

VII | THE GRACE OF GIVING

2 Corinthians 8

When we think of giving (in the context of believers), do we connect it with grace? Maybe, if we are the recipient! Paul takes a different slant. He starts off the discussion on the topic by bragging how the Churches in Macedonia had been graced by God to give in abundance, and with a rich generosity, because even in their severe trials and extreme poverty, they had a joy that overflowed to others (vs.1-2). Paul was there, and witnessed that they gave what they could, and more, without any persuasion! In fact, they begged Paul to take their gift, and fellowship with them in helping needy believers in Judea (vs.3-4; Acts 11:29-30).

Paul noted something even more important about these Macedonian Churches. Preceding their generous giving was their initial dedication to serve the Lord, and then to minister to Paul and Barnabas (v.5). So, he urged Titus, who had already started a 'Judea fund' at Corinth, to go and *"complete this grace"* in the Church there (v.6). As Paul writes, he compliments them on their great faith, as well as their excellence in speaking, their knowledge, diligence and love for the apostles. Then, *"See to it that you practice giving, so that you excel in this grace also"* (v.7)

Is giving a grace? Actually, in the original Greek, the same word, charis is used for both! I love Strong's definition – "the divine influence on the heart and its reflection in the life". And giving is one of the grace-gifts from the Father to the Church, listed in Rom.12:6-8. We need to practice it!

V.8 - There is no "Thou shalt give" order, but giving is an <u>indication of our love and gratitude to the Lord</u>. While we can learn about giving by following the example of others, our greatest example of giving is Jesus. Let these words penetrate your heart, and overwhelm you with love and thanksgiving: *"For you know the <u>grace</u> of our Lord Jesus Christ, that though He was rich, yet for your sakes He became poor, that you through His poverty might become rich"* (v. 9). Jesus, Himself, is God's gift to us! (2 Cor.9:15)

<u>Some practical advice about giving</u> – vs.10-14

- Be intentional about giving. Decide what you should give and to whom. (Ask God to show you!)
- Don't just think about it. Follow through with it.
- Don't give out of pressure, but willingly and gladly.
- You will not be judged for the amount you give. Give as you are able, not to match someone else's gift.
- The point of giving is not to impoverish yourself to ease the burden on someone else.
- You may give now to help someone in need, and when you are in want, you will receive from others, so there is equality, rather than 'feast or famine'.

To illustrate God's principle of equality, Paul quotes from Exod.16:18, in reference to the manna that came from heaven to feed the Israelites in the wilderness. It teaches trust in God as much as 'all being equal'. Some who were afraid the manna wouldn't keep coming, tried to hoard it, but what they didn't eat that day went moldy and wormy. Those who gathered little had no lack (Exod.16:20-25). On Friday they gathered for the Sabbath as well, and what they held over did not spoil. A lesson in trusting God!

Guarding the Gift — vs.16-24 — The topic of these verses indicates that there must have been some concern in the congregation: Would their large gift of money for the needy in Judea indeed get there and be used for its intended purpose? Sound familiar? Today, we supposedly have many checks and balances in place for accountability purposes, but we still hear stories of embezzlement and misuse of funds. As Paul intimates, the arrival and proper use of the gift depends more on the integrity and honor of those who handle it, than on the 'system'. Agreed?

Paul vouches for the integrity of Titus, and acknowledges that his reputation was very well established among the Churches, as was that of a second (unnamed) brother who also was chosen by the Church to accompany him. Paul did not want any blame to result, but that everything would be handled honorably in the sight of God and man. He does not seem concerned about thieves, thugs or other hazards along the way. He encourages the Church to take up the challenge, prove their love and not disappoint him.

Does the fact that tithing (10%) is not obligatory factor into my giving to the Church? What about charitable gifts and offerings above the tithe? Do I give out of gratitude for all God has given me, and done for me? Should I be giving, or giving more? Do I wonder: What's in it for me? Are these legitimate questions for a believer to ask?

VIII SOWING AND REAPING

2 Corinthians 9

Paul was obviously very conscientious about the proper administration of the 'benevolent fund' and delivering the gift to Judean believers. While applauding them for their willing-ness to give, and that their enthusiasm had spread to Achaia, he explains that he urged the brothers to go ahead of time to ensure that the gift has been prepared, and that it is ready to be dispatched on time, without them feeling pressured at the last minute (vs.1-5).

Principles of Giving – vs.6-7 – I think we all know the laws of sowing and reaping. Simply put: What you sow is what you reap, and the more you sow the more you reap, (with some provisos, such as weeds, which you don't sow, but they grow anyway; and a storm which can wipe out the harvest before you get a chance to reap, no matter how much you sowed). Paul explains that the same rules apply to giving and receiving. It's really our decision as to how much we give, but we should always give purposefully, and not with a begrudging attitude. Neither does the need necessarily dictate giving. God loves it when we give joyfully (that is, hilariously and without restraint). Hmmm. Sounds as if it might be fun!

Do I hear some of you thinking, "Well that lets me off the hook, because if we have to be cheerful about it (which I am not – I worked hard for that money, and I need it!), I will Scrooge my way through life, and let people with lots of money look after the poor"? Hmmm. Seems selfish.

The God of all grace - vs.8-11- Grace releases more grace! It is important to know that 1) God is the One whose grace *"abounds toward us."* Everything that is good in our life is a gift of God's grace, and 2) He is able to give us all we need, with some to spare, to share by means of gifts of grace to others (by good works). This was His plan for His people (Gen.12:2). Psa.112:9, quoted in v.9, reiterates this truth. 3) In the natural realm, God *"supplies seed to the sower, and bread for food."* 4) Therefore, we can expect that He will multiply the seed we have sown into someone else's life, so it is counted as righteous fruit in our lives, as well as 5) enriching us materially so we can share liberally, which 6) causes us to worship God with thanksgiving. In the end everybody is blessed! How good is *that*?

Vs.12-13 - By taking this gift from Corinth to Judea:

1) The needs of the saints are suppled,
2) There is a great chorus of praise to God,
3) Love is displayed, as believers are obedient,
4) God is praised for their witness and liberality,
5) The recipients pray God's added grace on them.

SO, (v.14) *"Thanks be to God* (who initiated this beautiful, multiplying, repetitive cycle of grace) *for His indescribable* (extravagant, unfathomable) *gift!"*

Grace is the gift that keeps on giving! Amen?

IX A SPIRITUAL WAR

2 Corinthians 10

Paul is working up to an issue that he soon has to address in his letter, and apologizes to the Corinth believers for his seeming schizophrenic moods. He admits acting like a teddy-bear when he's with them, but being as bold as a lion in his letters. Perhaps he hopes that his bold letters might deal with the problems, so that when he visits in person, he will be able to come "in the meekness and gentleness of Christ" (vs.1-2). It is going to take quite a while to lead up to addressing the real issue, but he wants them to be aware right off the top, that the reason there is trouble in the Church is because of the war. And he's not referring to a war fought with people in the natural world, though we may think it is (vs.1-3).

In reality it is a war fought in the spiritual realm, and it is fierce and relentless. We don't fight this war with metal swords or even with machine guns and rockets. Our weapons are provided by God and are mighty for pulling down strongholds - not fortresses built with stone and mortar on mountain tops, but strongholds in our mind. When we let the thoughts of the enemy capture our thinking, we become enslaved to his lies. The enemy we face is none other than Satan and his army of demons/evil spirits. Satan bombards our mind with lies that exalt him above the knowledge of God. With God's weapons, we can cast down his arguments, bringing every proud thought into captivity to the obedience of Christ (vs.4-5). Only then can we stand strong against him (v.6).

The spiritual war, and the armor which God provides us for the battle is described in detail in Eph.6:10-18. Every piece of God's mighty armor is provided to us as part of His "Salvation package". We need to put on the whole armor, so we can overcome the enemy in whatever way he attacks us. We also have the powerful name of Jesus and the blood of the cross to defeat him!

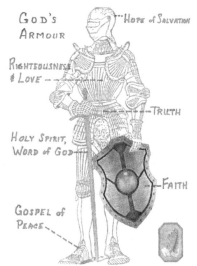

God's Armour — Hope of Salvation — Righteousness & Love — Truth — Holy Spirit, Word of God — Faith — Gospel of Peace

In another preamble, Paul needs to reiterate and confirm his authority as an Apostle. (10:7-8). He may not have appeared to be authoritative in his manner or stature, but being in Christ made him at least on a par with those in the Church. And he has an authority given to him by the Lord, not to put them down, but to build them up. He was not, nor should he have been ashamed of using boldness when confronting those co-operating with the enemy in bringing lies against him (v.8). He has to come against these lies, even if his tone frightens them (vs.9-11).

A God-appointed authority-12-18 - There are a few key phrases in v.12, often quoted and familiar to us: "*class ourselves, compare ourselves, commend themselves* and *measure themselves*". None of these 'self- appraisement' practices is wise! Paul says "*I dare not*" do this! To do so is a sign of either a spirit of pride or a spirit of inferiority. It is interesting that the outcome of comparison can end up either as self-commendation or self-condemnation. As to the former, "*he who glories, let him glory in the Lord, for not he who commends himself is approved, but whom the Lord commends*" (vs.17-18). As to the latter, "*there is now no condemnation to those in Christ* (Rom.8:1). Satan is the one who condemns us; let's not imitate him!

Vs. 13-16 speak to the authority God gave specifically to Paul, as an Apostle to the Gentiles. God had directed him to go to certain areas to establish Churches, while others spread the Gospel in other designated areas as the Lord led. Each place was a hub, from which they hoped the local Church would reach out to plant other Churches. Paul was careful not to use his authority in Churches outside his appointed jurisdiction, but to be faithful to preach the Word for the building up and growth of 'his own flock'. He did not boast in what he accomplished among them, but about their commitment to Christ and their love for others expressed in joyful giving.

What are some of Satan's tactics in his war against us?

How can we recognize the 'lies' of Satan?

What should we do when we recognize these lies?

X | FALSE TEACHERS

2 Corinthians 11:1-29; 12:11-19

Paul broaches a difficult subject by asking the readers of his letter to bear with him as he once again apologizes for having to use some heavy words (v.1). He wants them to know that he does this because of his passionate commitment to them. As their 'father in the faith', he has betrothed them to one husband, in order to present them to Christ as a chaste virgin (v.2; Eph.5:25-27). But as he talked about Satan previously, he expresses his concern that as Eve was deceived by Satan's craftiness, they might be turned away from the simple truth of the Gospel (v.3). This is a strong warning against being deceived by a different 'gospel', that preaches a different 'Jesus' (v.4).

Paul makes these points in showing the Church that <u>his credentials</u> stand up against those of any false prophet:

- While not as eloquent, <u>his knowledge</u> exceeds theirs.
- His knowledge has been made clear to the Church.
- He did not demand payment for ministry, but worked at a humble craft to support himself, and received money from other Churches to preach free of charge. This was so as <u>not</u> to be <u>burdensome to them</u>, and <u>because he loves them</u>.
- The Church will take abuse from these nefarious frauds, but don't appreciate Paul's <u>caring love</u>.
- Paul is an <u>Israelite</u>, <u>descendant of Abraham</u> and a <u>minister of Christ</u> as much as they are.
- Paul <u>preached the true Gospel of grace</u>.
- Paul has <u>suffered beatings, imprisonment, stoning and death for Christ and the Gospel</u>? Have they?
- Paul has <u>a deep concern for all the Churches</u>? Do they?
- Paul can <u>identify with the weak</u> and faltering. Do they?

- Paul <u>manifested the true</u> <u>*"signs of an apostle"*</u>. His ministry was marked by amazing <u>perseverance</u>, and <u>accompanied by signs, wonders and mighty deeds</u>.
- False prophets are deceitful workers, pretending to be apostles of Christ, (in order to take their money).
- They are like Satan, their leader, who comes in the guise of an angel of light to deceive God's people.
- Their deceitful works will be rewarded accordingly.

Paul was extremely protective of the Gospel, which he had received from Christ Himself. He was willing to defend it at all costs against any and all messengers who preached a corrupted version, or who would try to put the believers under Judaism (law as opposed to grace). Much of his letter to the Galatian Church is a defense of the pure Gospel which was being polluted and perverted by false teachers who wanted to bring the believers under the law (Gal.1:6-7). Note Paul's reaction to this in Gal.1:8-9 and 3:1-4. He was a true defender of the faith!

Do you think that the Gospel of Grace that Paul preached is still the same today, or has it been tampered with? Why do you think this?

XI PAUL'S SECRET

2 Corinthians 11:30-12:10

<u>The Basket Case</u> - "Some months ago, a strange incident was reported by witnesses returning to Jerusalem from Damascus, concerning a certain young man, a Pharisee, named Saul, from Tarsus. Sources tell us that Saul was on a special mission from the Sanhedrin to capture and incarcerate any one, man or woman, who was found to be a follower of 'The Way'. This is a cult that sprang up in the wake of the crucifixion of one Jesus, from Nazareth, for the dubious crime of blasphemy. Apparently the most noble Governor Pilate deferred to the request of the high priest to rid the world of this imposter who claimed to be the Son of God.

"Since the crucifixion, rumors have abounded that Jesus rose from the dead. Those who followed him have been propagating this rumor, and his teaching, so that their following now numbers in the thousands. As a devout and zealous Pharisee, Saul was appointed to head up a campaign to stop this insurrection before it escalated further. However, as he and the temple soldiers travelling with him approached Damascus on this mission, suddenly a blinding light, brighter than the mid-day sun, shone on Saul from the sky, and he fell to the ground. They heard a voice speaking to Saul, but saw no man. They led Saul, who was blinded by the light, into Damascus and left him there, returning to Jerusalem for further orders from the high priest.

"Recently another rumor claimed that Saul himself has become a member of 'The Way', even preaching in the synagogues in Damascus, saying that Jesus is the Christ, the Son of God. The Jews have been plotting to kill Saul, and have convinced the governor of Damascus to guard the city with a garrison of soldiers, to prevent Saul's escape, and arrest him. We will report more, when we receive news of Paul's capture . . . " Jerusalem Post

. . . Acts 9:23-25 – *"The Jews plotted to kill him, but their plot became known to Saul. And they watched the gates day and night, to kill him. Then the disciples took him by night and let him down through the wall in a large basket"*. (Story corroborated by Paul in his letter to the Church at Corinth, clarifying that he and his basket went through a window in the wall). Gal.1:17-18 tells us that Paul *"did not immediately confer with flesh and blood, nor go up to Jerusalem to those who were apostles but went to Arabia"*. Why Arabia? How long was he there? We don't have any clear answers. But if we look closely, we will find the answer to a mystery right here in 2 Cor.11.

Did you notice that just before Paul unexpectedly tells us about his basket escapade, he mentions boasting about his infirmity? And then comes yet another unexpected account, which undoubtedly reveals a secret that Paul had kept under wraps for many years. It explains a lot about Paul, and his amazing knowledge of God's salvation plan, something he certainly didn't learn in the Jewish synagogue, nor from the other apostles . . .

The Visit, the Visions and the Revelations - 12:1-7. Paul seems very tentative in telling us this story, as if he is not comfortable sharing it. He doesn't even admit that this seer of visions is he himself (just a man he knows, and *'such a one'*). He doesn't know if he actually left his body, or was bodily transported, but was *"caught up to the third heaven"*, *"into Paradise"*. And here's the kicker: "(*He*) i.e. I *heard inexpressible words, which it is not lawful for a man to utter.*" He had an "*abundance of revelations*". In v.7, Paul finally admits that the man whom he referenced is indeed himself. He says *"Lest I should be exalted above measure by the abundance of the revelations, a thorn in the flesh was given to me"*.

No wonder Paul's pen flowed with revelations of <u>hidden mysteries of the Godhead</u>, of <u>salvation truth</u>, of <u>the Church</u>, of <u>spiritual warfare</u> and of <u>things to come</u>. He packed his epistles with wisdom directly from the heart and mouth of Jesus, wisdom that Jesus did not teach His disciples, because they were not able to grasp it until after His resurrection and their baptism in the Holy Spirit. And Paul was a living, breathing demonstration of the power of this Gospel truth which he was commissioned to take to all the nations of the world. What an assignment!

We aren't told what the 'thorn in the flesh' was, probably by design. We can imagine it was constantly irritating, perhaps painful or embarrassing. What we *are* told is the <u>source,</u> and the <u>purpose</u>. Paul calls it *"a messenger of Satan to buffet me"*, like a pesky mosquito that keeps tormenting you with its constant buzzing reminders that you are weak and vulnerable, and it's out to get you.

The word 'torment' indicates that it could have been some sort of attack in the realm of the mind. Paul himself called it a weakness; somehow it kept him humble. This was the <u>purpose</u> of it: *"lest I be exalted above measure"*. It may possibly be the reason that he often apologized for how he presented himself. All speculation aside, it could not have been pleasant. Paul pleaded with the Lord three times to remove it from him (only three?) When the answer was NO, Paul accepted it, even gladly! It was a reminder to him that the power in him was not his own, but <u>the power of Christ resting on him</u> (12:7-9).

God's promise to Paul is one that has proven true for an innumerable number of believers over the centuries: "*My grace is sufficient for you, for My strength is made perfect in weakness.*" Paul proved it true, to the extent that he says "*I take pleasure in infirmities, in reproaches, in needs, in distresses, for Christ's sake, for when I am weak, then am I strong*" (vs.9-10).

The Word of God declares the theme of God's strength and our weakness repeatedly. Our weakness, or our lack of ability makes us a candidate to receive God's strength and grace to enable us to be and do all He has planned for us. He is not impressed with our ability; He wants our availability, and for His glory, He supplies the ability and enablement.

What word would you use to describe Paul?

XII FINAL COUNSEL & FAREWELL

2 Corinthians 12:14 - 13:14

Paul's emotions are all over the place in the closing words of this letter, as he sums up his message and adds warning and exhortation, before giving his gentle benediction. He announces his decision to make another visit, the third one, to the Corinthian Church. As before, he expects no remuneration or gifts, because as their father in the faith, he should be building into their future, not expecting them to support him. He is very happy to give his all for their spiritual well-being. His next wistful words sound like those of a mother of teen-agers: *"the more I love you, the less I am loved"*. Sadly true!

With a mixture of defensive statements and questions he reminds them of what he has already told them (16-19):

> I have never a burden to you, although I tricked you into
> giving by sending others to collect for the saints in Judea.
> Did I take advantage of you through them?
> Did Titus take advantage of you?
> Do not Titus and I have your best interest at heart?
> Do we have to make excuses for our actions?
> We are answerable to God, in Christ.
> We love you, and do everything to build you up!

Paul wants to make his expectations clear, so that when he sees them he will have no cause to fear any dispute, jealousy, anger, self-will, fault-finding, gossiping, pride or rebellion among them, or between him and them (v.20).

What exactly are Paul's expectations?

- 12:21 – Sincere repentance by those who still have not yet renounced and forsaken all sexual sins such as immoral living, fornication and lewd behavior.
- 13:5 – In light of their behavior, that they examine themselves to see if they really have Jesus living in them; and test the reality of their faith in Christ.

What can they expect if they do not comply and obey?

- 13:1-2 – Certain and severe disciplinary action.
- 13:3-4 – A demonstration of the power of Christ in him, and through him, to them.

Paul does not want to have to be heavy-handed with them. His desire is that through repentance of their sin they will be restored to fellowship with God, in holy living, filled with the strength of Christ in them, to grow in truth to maturity. His desire is to use his God-given authority for building them up, not tearing them down (13:5-10).

Receive the blessing of Paul's benediction in your heart:

Let Christ restore you and mature you in Him.
Let the Holy Spirit bring you comfort,
Live in peace, in Jesus, the Prince of Peace,
And the God of love and peace will be with you.
Show your love to one another in the Lord.
Stay in fellowship with other believers.
The Father's love, the grace and truth of the Son
And the communion of the Holy Spirit be with you!
Amen. (13:11-14)

OTHER BOOKS BY THIS AUTHOR
(Manuscript Review)

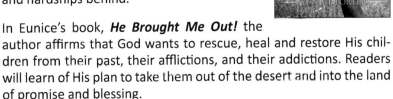

Title: HE BROUGHT ME OUT!
Author: Eunice Porter

This Xulon Book Helps Readers Jump Their Spiritual Hurdles

Eunice's book gives keys to leaving habits and hardships behind.

In Eunice's book, *He Brought Me Out!* the author affirms that God wants to rescue, heal and restore His children from their past, their afflictions, and their addictions. Readers will learn of His plan to take them out of the desert and into the land of promise and blessing.

"I hope that readers will be willing to let their lives be open before God, who wants so much for them to be free from fear, guilt and shame, and to live the abundant life Jesus gives," states the author. "I hope they will learn that repentance and sanctification are not outdated words, and that we can have victory over our thoughts, emotions and fears."

ISBN: 978 – 1 – 62419 – 854 – 0 / 5.5 X 8.5 / 183 pages

Reader Feedback

"In HE BROUHT ME OUT! Eunice has effectively communicated God's plan for each one of us with crystal clear clarity and succinctness. Well done!"–D

"It's like Christianity 101 – excellent for new believers, and for everyone!"– J

"It's loaded! Every paragraph is packed with truth. I like the unique humor that comes through to lighten the weighty words! – J

"My husband and I are going through your book together, a paragraph every morning, and looking up all the scriptures. We are learning a lot, and don't want to miss even a day!"

Title: KINGDOM LESSONS from the
Fabric of Life
Author: Eunice Porter

General Overview - Author
What I hope and pray is not that you remember the stories, or even learn from my foolish mistakes, but that you will let the lesson from the Word speak to your heart and change your life as it has changed mine.

Manuscript's Strengths - Review
- Voice is conversational, witty, achingly honest and deeply heartfelt. Each section is a pleasure to read.
- As the author points out, this is a work that functions equally well as a devotional, a teaching guide and an engaging testimony.
- Completely suitable for wholesale consumption during a couple of marathon reads, or for quick sips while sitting in a waiting room. This is an invaluable quality for this type of work. Well done.
- Associating each devotional with a snapshot slice of life serves several purposes: it aids internalization and retention of the lesson; lends weight by virtue of the author having lived it; and it simply makes for a smoother read, something that cannot be overrated.
- *[Editor's Note: "Ella May" was particularly moving. The image of the wooden box on the table will not soon leave me.]*

ISBN: 978 – 1 – 4984 – 1129 – 5 / 5.5 X 8.5 / 213 pages /Paperback

Reader Feedback

"KINGDOM LESSONS is a very valuable book. It is bringing great encouragement and inspiration. It has made me laugh and it has made me seek. Thank you, Eunice, for your obedience to the Lord to write this treasure." - T

"Thank you Eunice for KINGDOM LESSONS from the FABRIC OF LIFE. It's a real gem! God's Spirit has certainly gifted you and given you insight that is helpful to all who read what you have learned the easy way and the hard way." – RJ

Contact for all books: e-mail: eunique@telus.net
Website: euniceporter.com

CPSIA information can be obtained
at www.ICGtesting.com
Printed in the USA
LVOW02s0830220316

480156LV00007B/11/P